The CHASTISEMENT of the LORD

How The LORD Responds When Christians Sin

Kevin Madison

Copyright ©2021 Kevin Madison

All rights reserved. This book or any portion thereof may not be reproduced or used in any manner whatsoever without the express written permission of the publisher except for the use of brief quotations in a book review.

ISBN: 978-1-7377003-3-3 paperback
ISBN: 978-1-7377003-4-0 ebook

Cover design and publishing assistance by The Happy Self-Publisher

Published by Madison Christian Books, LLC
Kevin J. Madison
Founder: Treasure in Every Verse Ministry
Owner: Madison Christian Books, LLC
925 S. Lewis St. #255
New Iberia, LA 70560
Website: kevinjmadison.com
Email: tevm9328@gmail.com

To my parents, Pastor Leroy and Billie Mae Phillips: I cannot thank you both enough for introducing me to the Most High God. I cannot wait to worship before His throne with you, Dad. I am jealous you got there first. I miss you!

INTRODUCTION

Many believers struggle in their daily walk with the Lord. Life happens, as we are in the world yet not of it. Pilgrims, strangers, sheep, commanded to follow the Chief Shepard wherever he leads us. Along this path, the straight and narrow path, aligned with difficulties as the Lord prepares the table before us in the presence of our enemies. Then there are the natural sorrows accompanying a sin-plagued world hurling at light speed to its destruction.

The Lord Jesus testified of these things, declaring, "the kingdom of heaven suffers violence, and the violent take it by force." Thus, prophesying of the difficulties his children and servants will have in this fallen sin-stained world as we press forward in the kingdom of heaven.

In our frailties and moments of weakness, even we succumb to the dictates of our flesh or the temptations of the enemy.

What does our Lord see?

What does he know?

How will he respond when I go astray?

Can I be restored?

Will I be restored?

When, O Lord, will you come to my rescue?

Are you searching for the answer to these questions? Do you have a brother or sister in Christ who feels alienated from our Lord? Then look inside, as the answer to these questions and much more are discussed and explained in great detail.

"He that hath an ear let him hear."

CONTENTS

Introduction v

Part 1: Connecting the Chain Links 1

    Chapter 1: The Ancient Jewish Wedding 3

    Chapter 2: Christ and His Bride 13

    Chapter 3: The Wedding Supper of the Lamb 17

    Chapter 4: Wedding Guest and Judgment of the Nations . 23

    Chapter 5: Our Eternal Home 39

Part 2: The Seeker of Lost Sheep 49

    Chapter 1: Sheep and Goats 51

    Chapter 2: Lost and Found 61

    Chapter 3: From Corruption to Glory 65

Part 3: From Milk to Meat 73

    Chapter 1: The Perfect Candidate 75

    Chapter 2: The Terror of Hebrews 6 91

    Chapter 3: The Trepidation of Hebrews 10 115

    Chapter 4: The Torment of 2 Peter 2 133

Part 4: The Final Link in the Chain **153**
    Chapter 1: Jesus Inspects His Body 155
    Chapter 2: Disciplining the Church 187
    Chapter 3: The Sin unto Death. 193
    Chapter 4: Progression of the Lord's Discipline 199

PART 1

CONNECTING THE CHAIN LINKS

CHAPTER 1

THE ANCIENT JEWISH WEDDING

In an effort to enhance our understanding of the Word of God, certain principles should be considered. We are encouraged to do just that, as Paul states in **2 Tim. 2:15** "Study to shew thyself approved unto God, a workman who does not need to be ashamed, rightly dividing the word of truth."

There are primary principles that we should follow when studying the Bible as keys that enhance our understanding:

1. God's sovereign plan and providential will—how do the nation, people, and area being addressed fit in the reconciliation plan of God
2. Sacred history—everything happened sometime
3. Sacred geography—everything happened somewhere
4. Targeted audience—what did it mean to the people living at that time in that place
5. Targeted audience customs—historical traditions and rituals of the people being addressed
6. Reading the Bible through Jewish eyes—the Bible was written by Jews, about Jews, and primarily to Jews. Jesus is the Jewish Messiah.

A basic understanding of Jewish customs during the time when the biblical authors lived will vastly enhance one's understanding of the word of God and provide the subtext to the context of scripture.

For example, why were Joseph and Mary betrothed to one another yet not living together?

You may say: That is simple; they were only engaged, and the moral law of that day forbade such practice.

That is not entirely true. Engaged people have no need to file for a divorce.

In Jewish customs during Jesus' lifetime, once a couple became betrothed, they were legally married. During biblical days, the betrothal was the first of two steps in the marriage process. Betrothal legally binds the bride and the groom together in a marriage contract, except they do not physically live together.

The bride was usually chosen by the father of the bridegroom. The father would send his trusted servant, known as the agent of the father, to search out the bride. In Genesis 24, we read that Abraham (a type of God the Father) wishes to secure a bride for Isaac (a type of Messiah), so he sends his servant, Eliezer (a type of the Holy Spirit), to seek out a bride for his only son. The bride must first give her consent. Rebekah consented to marry Isaac before she ever met him. In like manner, today's believers in the Messiah consent to become the bride of Christ even though we have never seen Him.

Below is an extended excerpt from the Genesis account of Abraham sending Eliezer to retrieve Rebekah, the future wife of Isaac.

It is a little longer than the typical biblical excerpts used throughout this book, nevertheless extended for those who have never read the story or are currently without a copy of the Bible to provide proper context.

"[1] Abraham was now very old, and the LORD had blessed him in every way. [2] He said to the senior servant in his household, the one in charge of all that he had, "Put your hand under my thigh. [3] I want you to swear by the LORD, the God of heaven and the God of earth, that you will not get a wife for my son from the daughters of the Canaanites, among whom I am living, [4] but will go to my country and my own relatives and get a wife for my son Isaac." **Genesis 24:1-4**

[6] "Make sure that you do not take my son back there," Abraham said. [7] "The LORD, the God of heaven, who brought me out of my father's household and my native land and who spoke to me and promised me on oath, saying, 'To your offspring I will give this land' —he will send his angel before you so that you can get a wife for my son from there. **Genesis 24:6-7**

[12] Then he prayed, "LORD, God of my master Abraham, make me successful today, and show kindness to my master Abraham. [13] See, I am standing beside this spring, and the daughters of the townspeople are coming out to draw water. [14] May it be that when I say to a young woman, 'Please let down your jar that I may have a drink,' and she says, 'Drink, and I'll water your camels too' —let her be the one you have chosen for your servant Isaac. By this I will know that you have shown kindness to my master."

[15] Before he had finished praying, Rebekah came out with her jar on her shoulder. She was the daughter of Bethuel son of Milkah, who

was the wife of Abraham's brother Nahor. ¹⁶ The woman was very beautiful, a virgin; no man had ever slept with her. She went down to the spring, filled her jar and came up again. ¹⁷ The servant hurried to meet her and said, "Please give me a little water from your jar." ¹⁸ "Drink, my lord," she said, and quickly lowered the jar to her hands and gave him a drink. ¹⁹ After she had given him a drink, she said, "I'll draw water for your camels too, until they have had enough to drink." ²⁰ So she quickly emptied her jar into the trough, ran back to the well to draw more water, and drew enough for all his camels. ²¹ Without saying a word, the man watched her closely to learn whether or not the LORD had made his journey successful…²⁴ She answered him, "I am the daughter of Bethuel, the son that Milkah bore to Nahor. " ²⁵ And she added, "We have plenty of straw and fodder, as well as room for you to spend the night."

²⁶ Then the man bowed down and worshiped the LORD, ²⁷ saying, "Praise be to the LORD, the God of my master Abraham, who has not abandoned his kindness and faithfulness to my master. As for me, the LORD has led me on the journey to the house of my master's relatives."…³⁴ So he said, "I am Abraham's servant. ³⁵ The LORD has blessed my master abundantly, and he has become wealthy. He has given him sheep and cattle, silver and gold, male and female servants, and camels and donkeys. ³⁶ My master's wife Sarah has borne him a son in her old age, and he has given him everything he owns. ³⁷ And my master made me swear an oath, and said, 'You must not get a wife for my son from the daughters of the Canaanites, in whose land I live, ³⁸ but go to my father's family and to my own clan, and get a wife for my son.'

³⁹ "Then I asked my master, 'What if the woman will not come back with me?'

[40] "He replied, 'The LORD, before whom I have walked faithfully, will send his angel with you and make your journey a success, so that you can get a wife for my son from my own clan and from my father's family…[49] Now if you will show kindness and faithfulness to my master, tell me; and if not, tell me, so I may know which way to turn."

[50] Laban and Bethuel answered, "This is from the LORD; we can say nothing to you one way or the other. [51] Here is Rebekah; take her and go, and let her become the wife of your master's son, as the LORD has directed. " [52] When Abraham's servant heard what they said, he bowed down to the ground before the LORD. [53] Then the servant brought out gold and silver jewelry and articles of clothing and gave them to Rebekah; he also gave costly gifts to her brother and to her mother…[57] Then they said, "Let's call the young woman and ask her about it." [58] So they called Rebekah and asked her, "Will you go with this man?" "I will go," she said.

[59] So they sent their sister Rebekah on her way, along with her nurse and Abraham's servant and his men. [60] And they blessed Rebekah and said to her," **Genesis 24:12-60**

"[6] In all this you greatly rejoice, though now for a little while you may have had to suffer grief in all kinds of trials. [7] These have come so that the proven genuineness of your faith of greater worth than gold, which perishes even though refined by fire may result in praise, glory and honor when Jesus Christ is revealed. [8] Though you have not seen him, you love him; and even though you do not see him now, you believe in him and are filled with an inexpressible and glorious joy, [9] for you are receiving the end result of your faith, the salvation of your souls." **1 Peter 1:6-9**

The formality of the betrothal is completed when the groom presents valuable gifts to the bride, and she accepts them. This completed ritual is known in Hebrew as "kiddushin," which means "sanctification." The gifts to the bride are symbols of love, commitment, and loyalty. The gift God gives to those who accept Jesus is the Holy Spirit. When Jesus ascended to Heaven, He gave us gifts, including righteousness, eternal life, grace, faith, and other spiritual gifts. In addition, at this time, the cup of the covenant was shared and sealed between the bride and the groom with the drinking of wine. In doing so, the couple drinks from a common cup. The cup is first given to the groom to sip and then is given to the bride. Known as the cup of the covenant, this cup is spoken of by the prophet Jeremiah.

"[31] "Behold, the days are coming, says the LORD, when I will make a new covenant with the house of Israel and with the house of Judah— [32] not according to the covenant that I made with their fathers in the day that I took them by the hand to lead them out of the land of Egypt, My covenant which they broke, though I was a husband to them, says the LORD. [33] But this is the covenant that I will make with the house of Israel after those days, says the LORD: I will put My law in their minds, and write it on their hearts; and I will be their God, and they shall be My people. [34] No more shall every man teach his neighbor, and every man his brother, saying, 'Know the LORD,' for they all shall know Me, from the least of them to the greatest of them, says the LORD. For I will forgive their iniquity, and their sin I will remember no more." **Jeremiah 31:31-34**

The bride would then go through a ritual cleansing representing identification with the bridegroom and a break from her father's house and union with the bridegroom. This is a picture of water baptism and the baptism by the Holy Ghost transferring us from our natural father's house (Satan) into our Lord's Father's house (the LORD GOD).

The bridegroom would then depart for an indefinite period of time to make ready a place for them to live. Unlike our current society where the married couple would seek out their own place, the bridegroom, as given permission by his father, would add a room onto the father's house. The betrothed couple would not see each other again until the room was completed. However, the room was not declared complete until the father deemed it ready. Hence, the bridegroom nor the bride would ever truly know the exact wedding date. Both would live a life of expectation in faithfulness that today is the day of the bridegroom's return. Once the father gives the son his blessings for completing the room, the bridegroom, along with all the father's house, would go, in a wedding procession, to retrieve the bride and bring her home. This would typically happen at midnight with a shout from the wedding procession catching everyone along the procession route by surprise. The bridegroom would then take the bride out of her father's house and into the place that he had prepared. The bride and the groom would be in the wedding chamber for seven days. When the bride and the groom initially went into the wedding chamber, the friend of the bridegroom stood outside the door. All the assembled guests of the wedding gathered outside, waiting for the bridegroom's friend to announce the consummation of the marriage, which was relayed to him by the groom. John the Baptist referred to this in **John 3:29**. Upon notification, the wedding guests would all rejoice with singing and great joy.

"²⁹ The bride belongs to the bridegroom. The friend who attends the bridegroom waits and listens for him, and is full of joy when he hears the bridegroom's voice. That joy is mine, and it is now complete. ³⁰ He must become greater; I must become less." **John 3:29-30**

"And Jesus said unto them, Can the children of the bride chamber mourn, as long as the bridegroom is with them?" **Matthew 9:15**

The marriage was consummated on the first night. The bloodstained linen from this night was preserved. It was proof of the bride's virginity.

¹³ "If any man takes a wife, and goes in to her, and detests her, ¹⁴ and charges her with shameful conduct, and brings a bad name on her, and says, 'I took this woman, and when I came to her I found she was not a virgin,' ¹⁵ then the father and mother of the young woman shall take and bring out the evidence of the young woman's virginity to the elders of the city at the gate. ¹⁶ And the young woman's father shall say to the elders, 'I gave my daughter to this man as wife, and he detests her. ¹⁷ Now he has charged her with shameful conduct, saying, "I found your daughter was not a virgin," and yet these are the evidences of my daughter's virginity.' And they shall spread the cloth before the elders of the city. ¹⁸ Then the elders of that city shall take that man and punish him; ¹⁹ and they shall fine him one hundred shekels of silver and give them to the father of the young woman, because he has brought a bad name on a virgin of Israel. And she shall be his wife; he cannot divorce her all his days.

²⁰ "But if the thing is true, and evidences of virginity are not found for the young woman, ²¹ then they shall bring out the young

woman to the door of her father's house, and the men of her city shall stone her to death with stones, because she has done a disgraceful thing in Israel, to play the harlot in her father's house. So you shall put away the evil from among you. **Deuteronomy 22:13-21**

On the wedding day, the bridegroom is seen as a king and the bride as a queen. During the consummation of the marriage, the bridegroom will be crowned king, and his queen will rule with him for a lifetime.

CHAPTER 2

CHRIST AND HIS BRIDE

Oh beloved, what a wonderful and glorious picture of Christ and the Church. The Father sends the Holy Spirit to seek out a bridge for His only Son, Jesus. It is the role of the Holy Spirit to convict men of sin and lead them to God. Just as the bride was chosen by the bridegroom's father, so the believers in the Messiah are chosen by Father.

"35 And Jesus said to them, "I am the bread of life. He who comes to Me shall never hunger, and he who believes in Me shall never thirst. 36 But I said to you that you have seen Me and yet do not believe. 37 All that the Father gives Me will come to Me, and the one who comes to Me I will by no means cast out. 38 For I have come down from heaven, not to do My own will, but the will of Him who sent Me. 39 This is the will of the Father who sent Me, that of all He has given Me I should lose nothing, but should raise it up at the last day. 40 And this is the will of Him who sent Me, that everyone who sees the Son and believes in Him may have everlasting life; and I will raise him up at the last day." **John 6:35-40**

The bridegroom pours out his love upon the bride, and she reciprocates his love. They are joined in union as one throughout all eternity. All that belongs to the king now belongs to the queen.

"³¹ "For this reason a man shall leave his father and mother and be joined to his wife, and the two shall become one flesh." ³² This is a great mystery, but I speak concerning Christ and the church. ³³ Nevertheless let each one of you in particular so love his own wife as himself, and let the wife see that she respects her husband." **Ephesians 5:31-33**

"¹⁶You did not choose Me, but I chose you and appointed you that you should go and bear fruit, and that your fruit should remain, that whatever you ask the Father in My name He may give you. ¹⁷ These things I command you, that you love one another." **John 15:16-17**

Whenever you accept the Lord into your heart and life, you become betrothed to Him while living on earth. The payment offered was His life on the cross.

"⁴⁴No one can come to me unless the Father who sent me draws them, and I will raise them up at the last day. ⁴⁵ It is written in the Prophets: 'They will all be taught by God.' Everyone who has heard the Father and learned from him comes to me. ⁴⁶ No one has seen the Father except the one who is from God; only he has seen the Father. ⁴⁷ Very truly I tell you, the one who believes has eternal life. ⁴⁸ I am the bread of life. ⁴⁹ Your ancestors ate the manna in the wilderness, yet they died. ⁵⁰ But here is the bread that comes down from heaven, which anyone may eat and not die. ⁵¹ I am the living bread that came down from heaven. Whoever eats this bread will live forever. This bread is my flesh, which I will give for the life of the world." **John 6:44-51**

"⁴⁵For even the Son of Man did not come to be served, but to serve, and to give his life as a ransom for many." **Mark 10:45**

After the resurrection, Jesus returned to heaven to the Father's house to prepare a place (a room) for His bride, the Church.

"¹Do not let your hearts be troubled. You believe in God; believe also in me. ² My Father's house has many rooms; if that were not so, would I have told you that I am going there to prepare a place for you? ³ And if I go and prepare a place for you, I will come back and take you to be with me that you also may be where I am." **John 14:1-3**

In the fullness of time, when the rooms are ready, the Father will send the bridegroom, Jesus, back to the world to retrieve His bride, the Church.

"¹³Brothers and sisters, we do not want you to be uninformed about those who sleep in death, so that you do not grieve like the rest of mankind, who have no hope. ¹⁴ For we believe that Jesus died and rose again, and so we believe that God will bring with Jesus those who have fallen asleep in him. ¹⁵ According to the Lord's word, we tell you that we who are still alive, who are left until the coming of the Lord, will certainly not precede those who have fallen asleep. ¹⁶ For the Lord himself will come down from heaven, with a loud command, with the voice of the archangel and with the trumpet call of God, and the dead in Christ will rise first. ¹⁷ After that, we who are still alive and are left will be caught up together with them in the clouds to meet the Lord in the air. And so we will be with the Lord forever. ¹⁸ Therefore encourage one another with these words." **1 Thes. 4:13-18**

When Christ returns to heaven with His bride, all the inhabitants of heaven rejoice and worship before the throne of God in jubilant celebration. Then after the consummation, the second cup of the Covenant is offered by the bridegroom to the bride and invited guests. This was beautifully portrayed by the Lord in the upper room with His disciples after Judas Iscariot, the betrayer, departed the room.

"[17] Then He took the cup, and gave thanks, and said, "Take this and divide it among yourselves; [18] for I say to you, I will not drink of the fruit of the vine until the kingdom of God comes." [19] And He took bread, gave thanks and broke it, and gave it to them, saying, "This is My body which is given for you; do this in remembrance of Me." [20] Likewise He also took the cup after supper, saying, "This cup is the new covenant in My blood, which is shed for you." **Luke 22:17-20**

I can hardly contain my excitement, even so, come quickly, Lord Jesus! Amen.

CHAPTER 3

THE WEDDING SUPPER OF THE LAMB

When Jesus brings his bride, the Church, home to the Father's house, we will participate in the wedding supper of the Lamb during the great tribulation period, which is how long? Seven years. This coincides with Daniel's seventieth week of seven years, as mentioned in the book of Daniel in chapter 9. The final seven years is the final testing of Israel upon the earth to bring her back into a proper relationship with her husband, the Lord God. Hosea the prophet wrote an entire book concerning the relationship between God the Father and his wife, Israel. The prophets Jeremiah and Isaiah also spoke concerning the Father's relationship with Israel.

The final seven years of testing of Israel because of unfaithfulness to God is described in great detail by the prophet Zachariah in the 12th, 13th, and 14th chapters.

"² For I am jealous for you with godly jealousy. For I have betrothed you to one husband, that I may present you as a chaste virgin to Christ." **2 Corinthians 11:2**

"⁶Then I heard what sounded like a great multitude, like the roar of rushing waters and like loud peals of thunder, shouting:

"Hallelujah! For our Lord God Almighty reigns. ⁷ Let us rejoice and be glad and give him glory! For the wedding of the Lamb has come, and his bride has made herself ready. ⁸ Fine linen, bright and clean, was given her to wear." (Fine linen stands for the righteous acts of God's holy people.) ⁹ Then the angel said to me, "Write this: Blessed are those who are invited to the wedding supper of the Lamb!" And he added, "These are the true words of God." **Revelation 19:6-9**

"² "The kingdom of heaven is like a certain king who arranged a marriage for his son, ³ and sent out his servants to call those who were invited to the wedding; and they were not willing to come. ⁴ Again, he sent out other servants, saying, 'Tell those who are invited, "See, I have prepared my dinner; my oxen and fatted cattle are killed, and all things are ready. Come to the wedding." **Matthew 22:2-4**

"¹⁰ And while they went to buy, the bridegroom came, and those who were ready went in with him to the wedding; and the door was shut." **Matthew 25:10**

Israel, the Father's wife.

"¹¹ The LORD said to me, "Faithless Israel is more righteous than unfaithful Judah. ¹² Go, proclaim this message toward the north: "'Return, faithless Israel,' declares the LORD, 'I will frown on you no longer, for I am faithful,' declares the LORD, 'I will not be angry forever. ¹³ Only acknowledge your guilt you have rebelled against the LORD your God, you have scattered your favors to foreign gods under every spreading tree, and have not obeyed me,'" declares the LORD. ¹⁴ "Return, faithless people," declares the LORD, "for I am your husband. I will choose you one from a town and two from a clan and bring you to Zion." **Jeremiah 3:11-14**

"5 For your Maker is your husband the LORD Almighty is his name the Holy One of Israel is your Redeemer; he is called the God of all the earth. 6 The LORD will call you back as if you were a wife deserted and distressed in spirit a wife who married young, only to be rejected," says your God. 7 "For a brief moment I abandoned you, but with deep compassion I will bring you back. 8 In a surge of anger I hid my face from you for a moment, but with everlasting kindness I will have compassion on you," says the LORD your Redeemer. 9 "To me this is like the days of Noah, when I swore that the waters of Noah would never again cover the earth. So now I have sworn not to be angry with you, never to rebuke you again.10 Though the mountains be shaken and the hills be removed, yet my unfailing love for you will not be shaken nor my covenant of peace be removed," says the LORD, who has compassion on you." **Isaiah 54:5-10**

The prophet Daniel spoke extensively concerning the final seven years of human history upon the earth during the church age. The church age is defined as the duration of years from the resurrection of Jesus until the rapture of the true church, the body of Christ. When I say church, it is not a reference to an organization, denomination, culture, race, creed, or nation. The true church is made up of born-again believers in Christ who possess the presence of the Holy Spirit in them from all people, nations, and tongues. Daniel's prophecy gives us the timeline of major events that take place during these seven years of tribulation upon the earth while the church celebrates and worships the Lord who sits upon the throne in heaven.

"**20** While I was speaking and praying, confessing my sin and the sin of my people Israel and making my request to the LORD my God for his holy hill **21** while I was still in prayer, Gabriel, the man I had seen in the earlier vision, came to me in swift flight about the time of the evening sacrifice. **22** He instructed me and said to me, "Daniel, I have now come to give you insight and understanding. **23** As soon as you began to pray, a word went out, which I have come to tell you, for you are highly esteemed. Therefore, consider the word and understand the vision: **24** "Seventy 'sevens' are decreed for your people and your holy city to finish transgression, to put an end to sin, to atone for wickedness, to bring in everlasting righteousness, to seal up vision and prophecy and to anoint the Most Holy Place. **25** "Know and understand this: From the time the word goes out to restore and rebuild Jerusalem until the Anointed One, the ruler, comes, there will be seven 'sevens,' and sixty-two 'sevens.' It will be rebuilt with streets and a trench, but in times of trouble. **26** After the sixty-two 'sevens,' the Anointed One will be put to death and will have nothing. The people of the ruler who will come will destroy the city and the sanctuary. The end will come like a flood: War will continue until the end, and desolations have been decreed. **27** He will confirm a covenant with many for one 'seven.' In the middle of the 'seven' he will put an end to sacrifice and offering. And at the temple he will set up an abomination that causes desolation, until the end that is decreed is poured out on him." **Daniel 9:20-27**

The Lord Jesus spoke of this seven-year period of time, giving the description known by even the casual Bible prophesy reader, the great tribulation. Note that the "great tribulation" is designated as the final three-and-one-half years of the seven-year period.

"³⁵ "Let your waist be girded and your lamps burning; ³⁶ and you yourselves be like men who wait for their master, when he will return from the wedding, that when he comes and knocks they may open to him immediately. ³⁷ Blessed are those servants whom the master, when he comes, will find watching. Assuredly, I say to you that he will gird himself and have them sit down to eat, and will come and serve them. ³⁸ And if he should come in the second watch, or come in the third watch, and find them so, blessed are those servants. ³⁹ But know this, that if the master of the house had known what hour the thief would come, he would have watched and not allowed his house to be broken into. ⁴⁰ Therefore you also be ready, for the Son of Man is coming at an hour you do not expect." **Luke 12:35-40**

In the parable above, Jesus is speaking to his disciples in private when he states when he (Jesus) will return from the wedding (to the church).

You may be asking: Return to where?

Planet earth.

Why would he do that?

Because the Father wants his wife back and the saved remnants of Israel are the guests of honor to the wedding feast, which will last for 1,000 years.

Wow, are we going to have some fun celebrating and ruling over the earth with the King.

CHAPTER 4

WEDDING GUEST AND JUDGMENT OF THE NATIONS

In the previous chapter, we learned that our Lord, Jesus Christ, has a bride named the Church. We also learned that the two were wedded in heaven over a seven-year period while the inhabitants of the earth are plagued with the wrath of God, and Israel is burdened with severe persecution by the devil and his cohorts until she is nearly extinguished. With only one-third of her people surviving the genocide, the remnant of Israel finally calls upon Jesus, their true King, to save them. Upon hearing their repentant call, the Lord Jesus turns out all the natural lights of heaven, then steps out of the spiritual realm into the physical realm revealing that He is, in fact, the Most High God. All the remaining inhabitants of the earth and the army of the antichrist prepare themselves to commence war against the Lord, who is followed by all the church, Old Testament saints, and all the angels of heaven, all upon white horses.

"[11] Now I saw heaven opened, and behold, a white horse. And He who sat on him was called Faithful and True, and in righteousness, He judges and makes war. [12] His eyes were like a flame of fire, and on His head were many crowns. He had a name written that no one knew except Himself. ¹³ He was clothed with a robe dipped in blood, and His name is called The Word of God. ¹⁴ And the armies in heaven, clothed in fine linen, white and clean, followed Him on white horses. ¹⁵ Now out of His mouth goes a sharp sword, that with it He should strike the nations. And He Himself will rule them with a rod of iron. He Himself treads the winepress of the fierceness and wrath of Almighty God. ¹⁶ And He has on His robe and on His thigh a name written: KING OF KINGS AND LORD OF LORDS." **Revelation 19:11-16**

"¹⁷ Then I saw an angel standing in the sun; and he cried with a loud voice, saying to all the birds that fly in the midst of heaven, "Come and gather together for the supper of the great God, ¹⁸ that you may eat the flesh of kings, the flesh of captains, the flesh of mighty men, the flesh of horses and of those who sit on them, and the flesh of all people, free and slave, both small and great."¹⁹ And I saw the beast, the kings of the earth, and their armies, gathered together to make war against Him who sat on the horse and against His army. ²⁰ Then the beast was captured, and with him the false prophet who worked signs in his presence, by which he deceived those who received the mark of the beast and those who worshiped his image. These two were cast alive into the lake of fire burning with brimstone. ²¹ And the rest were killed with the sword which proceeded from the mouth of Him who sat on the horse. And all the birds were filled with their flesh." **Revelation 19:17-21**

"¹³ "I was watching in the night visions, and behold, One like the Son of Man, Coming with the clouds of heaven! He came to the Ancient of Days, and they brought Him near before Him. ¹⁴ Then to Him was given dominion and glory and a kingdom, that all peoples, nations, and languages should serve Him. His dominion is an everlasting dominion, which shall not pass away, and His kingdom the one which shall not be destroyed." **Daniel 7:13-14**

The battle will not last long as the Lord quickly destroys the armies of the world with a spoken word. When the Lord returns, his feet will land upon the top of the Mount of Olives. The remnant of Israel will flee into the valley as the mountain split in two at the presence of the Most High God.

"¹ A Day of the LORD is coming, Jerusalem, when your possessions will be plundered and divided up within your very walls. ² I will gather all the nations to Jerusalem to fight against it; the city will be captured, the houses ransacked, and the women raped. Half of the city will go into exile, but the rest of the people will not be taken from the city. ³ Then the LORD will go out and fight against those nations, as he fights on a day of battle. ⁴ On that day his feet will stand on the Mount of Olives, east of Jerusalem, and the Mount of Olives will be split in two from east to west, forming a great valley, with half of the mountain moving north and half moving south. ⁵ You will flee by my mountain valley, for it will extend to Azel. You will flee as you fled from the earthquake in the days of Uzziah king of Judah. Then the LORD my God will come, and all the holy ones with him. ⁶ On that day there will be neither sunlight nor cold, frosty darkness. ⁷ It will be a unique day a day known only to the LORD with no distinction between day and night. When evening comes, there will be light." **Zechariah 14:1-7**

Please understand that Israel is not the Church, and the Church is not Israel. If you confuse this issue, it will be very difficult to understand the prophecies written in the word of God. God has a distinct plan for each entity. Furthermore, Israel is the Father's wife, and the Church is the Son's bride. As mentioned previously, this pictured perfectly with Abraham selecting Rebecca as a bride for his only Son, Isaac. The Lord's plan for Israel cannot be annulled. In fact, the Lord has declared that Israel will forever be a nation before him.

"[31] "The days are coming," declares the LORD, "when I will make a new covenant with the people of Israel and with the people of Judah. [32] It will not be like the covenant I made with their ancestors when I took them by the hand to lead them out of Egypt, because they broke my covenant, though I was a husband to them," declares the LORD. [33] "This is the covenant I will make with the people of Israel after that time," declares the LORD. "I will put my law in their minds and write it on their hearts. I will be their God, and they will be my people. [34] No longer will they teach their neighbor, or say to one another, 'Know the LORD,' because they will all know me, from the least of them to the greatest," declares the LORD.

"For I will forgive their wickedness and will remember their sins no more." [35] This is what the LORD says, he who appoints the sun to shine by day, who decrees the moon and stars to shine by night, who stirs up the sea so that its waves roar the LORD Almighty is his name:

[36] "Only if these decrees vanish from my sight," declares the LORD, "will Israel ever cease being a nation before me." [37] This is what the LORD says: "Only if the heavens above can be measured and the foundations of the earth below be searched out will I reject all the descendants of Israel because of all they have done," declares the LORD." **Jeremiah 31:31-37**

[7] "The LORD will save the dwellings of Judah first, so that the honor of the house of David and of Jerusalem's inhabitants may not be greater than that of Judah. [8] On that day the LORD will shield those who live in Jerusalem, so that the feeblest among them will be like David, and the house of David will be like God, like the angel of the LORD going before them. [9] On that day I will set out to destroy all the nations that attack Jerusalem. [10] "And I will pour out on the house of David and the inhabitants of Jerusalem a spirit of grace and supplication. They will look on me, the one they have pierced, and they will mourn for him as one mourns for an only child and grieve bitterly for him as one grieves for a firstborn son. [11] On that day the weeping in Jerusalem will be as great as the weeping of Hadad Rimmon in the plain of Megiddo. [12] The land will mourn, each clan by itself, with their wives by themselves: the clan of the house of David and their wives, the clan of the house of Nathan and their wives, [13] the clan of the house of Levi and their wives, the clan of Shimei and their wives, [14] and all the rest of the clans and their wives. [1] "On that day a fountain will be opened to the house of David and the inhabitants of Jerusalem, to cleanse them from sin and impurity.

[2] "On that day, I will banish the names of the idols from the land, and they will be remembered no more," declares the LORD Almighty. "I will remove both the prophets and the spirit of impurity from the land. **Zechariah 12:7-13:2**

"[19] "The sun shall no longer be your light by day, Nor for brightness shall the moon give light to you; But the LORD will be to you an everlasting light, And your God your glory. [20] Your sun shall no longer go down, Nor shall your moon withdraw itself; For the LORD will be your everlasting light, And the days of your mourning shall be ended. [21] Also your people shall all be righteous; They shall inherit the land forever, The branch of My planting, The work of My hands, That I may be glorified. [22] A little one shall become a thousand, And a small one a strong nation. I, the LORD, will hasten it in its time." **Isaiah 60:19-22**

Although Israel was unfaithful, the Lord declared that he will take her back and cleanse her from her filthiness.

"[31] "You erected your shrine at the head of every road, and built your high place in every street. Yet you were not like a harlot, because you scorned payment. [32] You are an adulterous wife, who takes strangers instead of her husband. [33] Men make payment to all harlots, but you made your payments to all your lovers, and hired them to come to you from all around for your harlotry. [34] You are the opposite of other women in your harlotry, because no one solicited you to be a harlot. In that you gave payment but no payment was given you, therefore you are the opposite." **Ezekiel 16:31-34**

"[20] Surely, as a wife treacherously departs from her husband, So have you dealt treacherously with Me, O house of Israel," says the LORD." **Jeremiah 3:20**

"[8] And it shall be in that day, that living waters shall go out from Jerusalem; half of them toward the former sea, and half of them toward the hinder sea: in summer and in winter shall it be. [9] And the LORD shall be king over all the earth: in that day shall there be one LORD, and his name one. [10] All the land shall be turned as a plain from Geba to Rimmon south of Jerusalem: and it shall be lifted up, and inhabited in her place, from Benjamin's gate unto the place of the first gate, unto the corner gate, and from the tower of Hananeel unto the king's winepresses. [11] And men shall dwell in it, and there shall be no more utter destruction; but Jerusalem shall be safely inhabited." **Zechariah 14:8-11**

Immediately after the seven years of tribulation upon the earth, the Lord Jesus returns to establish His Kingdom upon the earth, which will last for 1,000 years. This is not the rapture of the church. Remember, the Lord took the church off the earth prior to the commencement of the seven-year tribulation period. This is clearly seen in Revelation 4 and 5 as we see the church on earth in chapters 2 and 3, then worshipping around the throne in the next two chapters. This is the second coming of the Jewish Messiah in response to the Jews finally acknowledging Jesus as their Savior, Lord, and God.

"[29] "Immediately after the tribulation of those days the sun will be darkened, and the moon will not give its light; the stars will fall from heaven, and the powers of the heavens will be shaken. [30] Then the sign of the Son of Man will appear in heaven, and then all the tribes of the earth will mourn, and they will see the Son of Man coming on the clouds of heaven with power and great glory. [31] And He will send His angels with a great sound of a trumpet, and they will gather together His elect from the four winds, from one end of heaven to the other." **Matthew 24:29-31**

The believers are welcomed into the kingdom because they are believers and were expecting the return of the Messiah and King. These believers include both Jews and Gentiles.

"[10]When Jesus heard this, he was amazed and said to those following him, "Truly I tell you, I have not found anyone in Israel with such great faith. [11] I say to you that many will come from the east and the west and will take their places at the feast with Abraham, Isaac and Jacob in the kingdom of heaven." **Mat. 8:10-11**

Now let us read **Matthew 25:1-13** concerning the ten virgins. I want to remind you once again, this is not the rapture of the church but a future event involving the angels of God gathering all the believers in Christ after the tribulation from amongst all nations of the world, especially Jewish believers. These people survived the horrors and judgments for the past seven years. What a story they will have for their children and grandchildren! The parable below gives a picture that states only 50% of all those survivors are true believers in Christ. Therefore, the Millennium will commence with only a few hundred million people in their natural bodies.

[1] "At that time the kingdom of heaven will be like ten virgins who took their lamps and went out to meet the bridegroom. [2] Five of them were foolish and five were wise. [3] The foolish ones took their lamps but did not take any oil with them. [4] The wise ones, however, took oil in jars along with their lamps. [5] The bridegroom was a long time in coming, and they all became drowsy and fell asleep. [6] "At midnight the cry rang out: 'Here's the bridegroom! Come out to meet him!' [7] "Then all the virgins woke up and trimmed their lamps. [8] The foolish ones said to the wise, 'Give us some of your oil; our lamps are going out.' [9] "'No,' they replied, 'there may not be enough for both us and you. Instead, go to those who sell oil and buy some for yourselves.' [10] "But while they were on their way to buy the oil, the bridegroom arrived. The virgins who were ready went in with him to the wedding banquet. And the door was shut.

[11] "Later the others also came. 'Lord, Lord,' they said, 'open the door for us!' [12] "But he replied, 'Truly I tell you, I don't know you.' [13] "Therefore keep watch, because you do not know the day or the hour." **Matthew 25:1-13**

This happens after the rapture of the Church and after the great tribulation. Jesus has returned to the earth with the Church and all the angels to rule on the throne of David from Jerusalem. There are believers and unbelievers, both Jews and Gentiles, who have made it through the great tribulation in their natural bodies. Of approximately 7 to 8 billion people living on earth, approximately fewer than 500 million people are alive. Nevertheless, out of these 500 million people, only a portion are believers, and the others are unbelievers, some with the mark of the beast. One group has the oil, that is, the Spirit of God, and the other group does not. That is how Jesus identified which ones were truly believers. They had His seal.

"¹ Then I heard him call out in a loud voice, "Bring near those who are appointed to execute judgment on the city, each with a weapon in his hand." ² And I saw six men coming from the direction of the upper gate, which faces north, each with a deadly weapon in his hand. With them was a man clothed in linen who had a writing kit at his side. They came in and stood beside the bronze altar. ³ Now the glory of the God of Israel went up from above the cherubim, where it had been, and moved to the threshold of the temple. Then the LORD called to the man clothed in linen who had the writing kit at his side ⁴ and said to him, "Go throughout the city of Jerusalem and **put a mark on the foreheads of those who grieve and lament over all the detestable things that are done in it.**" **Ezekiel 9:1-4**

"¹³When you believed, **you were marked in him with a seal, the promised Holy Spirit,** ¹⁴who is a deposit guaranteeing our inheritance until the redemption (gathering) of those **who are God's possession** to the praise of his glory." **Ephesians 1:13-14**

"²¹ Now it is God who makes both us and you stand firm in Christ. **He anointed us,** ²² **set his seal of ownership on us, and put** his Spirit in our hearts as a deposit, guaranteeing what is to come." **2 Corinthians 1:21-22**

"³⁰ And do not grieve the Holy Spirit of God, with whom **you were sealed for the day of redemption.**" **Ephesians 4:30**

"¹⁹ Nevertheless, God's solid foundation stands firm, **sealed with this inscription: "The Lord knows those who are his**," and, "Everyone who confesses the name of the Lord must turn away from wickedness." **2 Timothy 2:19**

³ "Do not harm the land or the sea or the trees **until we put a seal on the foreheads of the servants of our God." Revelation 7:3**

The others are unbelievers that were not expecting Jesus to return. They are judged immediately, die immediately, and sent to Hades, the temporary holding jail cell for 1,000 years until the Great White Throne Judgment Day.

"¹⁰ When Jesus heard it, He marveled, and said to those who followed, "Assuredly, I say to you, I have not found such great faith, not even in Israel! ¹¹ And I say to you that many will come from east and west, and sit down with Abraham, Isaac, and Jacob in the kingdom of heaven. ¹² But the sons of the kingdom will be cast out into outer darkness. There will be weeping and gnashing of teeth." **Matthew 8:10-12**

Gentiles in the kingdom of Christ with Abraham will enjoy salvation and the blessing of God. The Jewish nation, physical heirs of Abraham through Isaac and Jacob, who chose not to believe, will be cast out. This was exactly opposite to the rabbinical understanding, which suggested that the kingdom would feature a great feast in the company of Abraham and the Messiah open to Jews only. That interpretation does not align with scripture in the Old or New Testaments, and the unbelieving Jew will be cast into outer darkness where there will be weeping and gnashing of teeth. This expression describes the eternal agonies of those in hell.

"[30]And throw that worthless servant outside, into the outer darkness, where there will be weeping and gnashing of teeth.'" **Matthew 25:30**

This same principle is applied to the nations. This is the parable given by the Lord Jesus about the judgment of the sheep and goats nations after the second coming.

[31] "When the Son of Man comes in his glory, and all the angels with him, he will sit on his glorious throne. [32] All the nations will be gathered before him, and he will separate the people one from another as a shepherd separates the sheep from the goats. [33] He will put the sheep on his right and the goats on his left. [34] "Then the King will say to those on his right, 'Come, you who are blessed by my Father; take your inheritance, the kingdom prepared for you since the creation of the world. [35] For I was hungry and you gave me something to eat, I was thirsty and you gave me something to drink, I was a stranger and you invited me in, [36] I needed clothes and you clothed me, I was sick and you looked after me, I was in prison and you came to visit me.'

[37] "Then the righteous will answer him, 'Lord, when did we see you hungry and feed you, or thirsty and give you something to drink? [38] When did we see you a stranger and invite you in, or needing clothes and clothe you? [39] When did we see you sick or in prison and go to visit you?'

⁴⁰ "The King will reply, 'Truly I tell you, whatever you did for one of the least of these brothers and sisters of mine, you did for me.' ⁴¹ "Then he will say to those on his left, 'Depart from me, you who are cursed, into the eternal fire prepared for the devil and his angels. ⁴² For I was hungry and you gave me nothing to eat, I was thirsty and you gave me nothing to drink, ⁴³ I was a stranger and you did not invite me in, I needed clothes and you did not clothe me, I was sick and in prison and you did not look after me.' ⁴⁴ "They also will answer, 'Lord, when did we see you hungry or thirsty or a stranger or needing clothes or sick or in prison, and did not help you?'

⁴⁵ "He will reply, 'Truly I tell you, whatever you did not do for one of the least of these, you did not do for me.' ⁴⁶ "Then they will go away to eternal punishment, but the righteous to eternal life." **Matthew 25:31-46**

They will be judged based on how they treated the 144,000 Jewish missionaries sealed by the Lord to preach the gospel to every tribe, nation, and tongue during the tribulation.

"³Do not harm the land or the sea or the trees until we put a seal on the foreheads of the servants of our God." ⁴ Then I heard the number of those who were sealed: 144,000 from all the tribes of Israel." **Revelation 7:3-4**

The two witnesses, "³And I will appoint my two witnesses, and they will prophesy for 1,260 days, clothed in sackcloth." ⁴ They are "the two olive trees" and the two lampstands, and "they stand before the Lord of the earth." ⁵ If anyone tries to harm them, fire comes from their mouths and devours their enemies. This is how anyone who wants to harm them must die. ⁶ They have power to shut up the heavens so that it will not rain during the time they are prophesying; and they have power to turn the waters into blood and to strike the earth with every kind of plague as often as they want." **Revelation 11:3-7**

And those who receive Christ as Savior during the great tribulation, "⁹When he opened the fifth seal, I saw under the altar the souls of those who had been slain because of the word of God and the testimony they had maintained. ¹⁰ They called out in a loud voice, "How long, Sovereign Lord, holy and true, until you judge the inhabitants of the earth and avenge our blood?" ¹¹ Then each of them was given a white robe, and they were told to wait a little longer, until the full number of their fellow servants, their brothers and sisters, were killed just as they had been." **Revelation 6:9-11**

"⁴I saw thrones on which were seated those who had been given authority to judge. And I saw the souls of those who had been beheaded because of their testimony about Jesus and because of the word of God. They had not worshiped the beast or its image and had not received its mark on their foreheads or their hands. They came to life and reigned with Christ a thousand years. ⁵ (The rest of the dead did not come to life until the thousand years were ended.) This is the first resurrection. ⁶ Blessed and holy are those who share in the first resurrection. The second death has no power over them, but they will be priests of God and of Christ and will reign with him for a thousand years." **Revelation 20:4-6**

There will be no comfort for anyone who rejects God's free gift of salvation purchased for all through the blood of the cross of Christ. No excuse will be acceptable as the Father has given everyone the laws of God written on their hearts, our conscience bearing us witness and the full revelation as testified by creation. You do not want to be included in this group.

"¹⁸ The wrath of God is being revealed from heaven against all the godlessness and wickedness of people, who suppress the truth by their wickedness, ¹⁹ since what may be known about God is plain to them, because God has made it plain to them. ²⁰ For since the creation of the world God's invisible qualities—his eternal power and divine nature—have been clearly seen, being understood from what has been made, so that people are without excuse.

²¹ For although they knew God, they neither glorified him as God nor gave thanks to him, but their thinking became futile, and their foolish hearts were darkened. ²² Although they claimed to be wise, they became fools ²³ and exchanged the glory of the immortal God for images made to look like a mortal human being and birds and animals and reptiles." **Romans 1:18-23**

In the end, all the enemies of Christ will be given a fair trial and judged according to their works. They will quickly find out that their works (behaviors) are not sufficient to satisfy the righteous indignation of a Holy God. All who have rejected Christ will be denied entry into the kingdom and forever consigned to the life they desired, which is a life without God. Unfortunately, this life will consist of burning forever without the ability to die in the lake of fire filled with brimstone where the worm never dies, and the fire is not quenched. They will join the devil, the antichrist, and the false prophet, in the pit where there will be weeping and gnashing of teeth.

"⁶ Blessed and holy are those who share in the first resurrection. The second death has no power over them, but they will be priests of God and of Christ and will reign with him for a thousand years.

The Judgment of Satan ⁷ When the thousand years are over, Satan will be released from his prison ⁸ and will go out to deceive the nations in the four corners of the earth Gog and Magog and to gather them for battle. In number they are like the sand on the seashore. ⁹ They marched across the breadth of the earth and surrounded the camp of God's people, the city he loves. But fire came down from heaven and devoured them. ¹⁰ And the devil, who deceived them, was thrown into the lake of burning sulfur, where the beast and the false prophet had been thrown. They will be tormented day and night for ever and ever." **Revelation 20:6-10**

"¹¹ Then I saw a great white throne and him who was seated on it. The earth and the heavens fled from his presence, and there was no place for them. ¹² And I saw the dead, great and small, standing before the throne, and books were opened. Another book was opened, which is the book of life. The dead were judged according to what they had done as recorded in the books. ¹³ The sea gave up the dead that were in it, and death and Hades gave up the dead that were in them, and each person was judged according to what they had done. ¹⁴ Then death and Hades were thrown into the lake of fire. The lake of fire is the second death. ¹⁵ Anyone whose name was not found written in the book of life was thrown into the lake of fire." **Revelation 20:11-15**

CHAPTER 5

The Church's Eternal Home

Since we ended chapter 4 with an overview of the fate that awaits those who reject the reconciliation offered by God through faith in His Son, the Lord Jesus Christ, let us together venture into the future abode of the church. Even the most casual of Bible readers may remember the verse below due to the unfortunate translation in the King James Version of the Bible, "many mansions." The Greek word used in this passage is "mone," which literally means dwelling. The definition of mansions varies from person to person and nation to nation. However, everyone has the same definition of a dwelling place. This goes back to the story of the Jewish wedding whereby the bridegroom is adding on to the Father's house. The house belongs to the Father, and each of His children receives a room. Fortunately for us, the church, we will have a glorified body fashioned after our Lord's resurrected body as detailed by Paul in **1 Cor. 15** and noted by John in **1 John 3**.

"[47] The first man was of the earth, made of dust; the second Man is the Lord from heaven. [48] As was the man of dust, so also are those who are made of dust; and as is the heavenly Man, so also are those who are heavenly. [49] And as we have borne the image of the man of dust, we shall also bear the image of the heavenly Man.

⁵⁰ Now this I say, brethren, that flesh and blood cannot inherit the kingdom of God; nor does corruption inherit incorruption. ⁵¹ Behold, I tell you a mystery: We shall not all sleep, but we shall all be changed— ⁵² in a moment, in the twinkling of an eye, at the last trumpet. For the trumpet will sound, and the dead will be raised incorruptible, and we shall be changed. ⁵³ For this corruptible must put on incorruption, and this mortal must put on immortality. ⁵⁴ So when this corruptible has put on incorruption, and this mortal has put on immortality, then shall be brought to pass the saying that is written: "Death is swallowed up in victory." ⁵⁵ "O Death, where is your sting? O Hades, where is your victory?" **1 Corinthians 15:47-55**

"² Beloved, now we are children of God; and it has not yet been revealed what we shall be, but we know that when He is revealed, we shall be like Him, for we shall see Him as He is. ³ And everyone who has this hope in Him purifies himself, just as He is pure." **1 John 3:2-3**

"¹ "Do not let your hearts be troubled. You believe in God; believe also in me. ² My Father's house has many rooms; if that were not so, would I have told you that I am going there to prepare a place for you? ³ And if I go and prepare a place for you, I will come back and take you to be with me that you also may be where I am. ⁴ You know the way to the place where I am going." **John 14:1-4**

The entire 14th chapter of the book of John presents Christ as the One who gives the believer comfort while residing on earth through the ministry of the Holy Spirit. It also describes precious promises of eternal rest and comfort upon His future return for His bride. This discussion took place in the upper room after Judas Iscariot, the betrayer, departed with His disciples prior to Jesus' arrest.

The disciples noticed the change in Jesus' demeanor and tone as He set his sights on the cross where the weight of every sin ever committed in heaven and on the earth will be placed upon His back by the Father. Even more troubling for our Lord was the pending separation from the Father and the Holy Spirit with whom He is One. There was no fear of dying in Jesus as He is perfect love and was pleased to do the Father's will.

"[28] Then Jesus said to them, "When you lift up the Son of Man, then you will know that I am He, and that I do nothing of Myself; but as My Father taught Me, I speak these things. [29] And He who sent Me is with Me. The Father has not left Me alone, for I always do those things that please Him." **John 8:28-29**

Likewise, it is written by Isaiah the prophet, "[10] Yet it pleased the LORD to bruise Him; He has put Him to grief. When You make His soul an offering for sin, He shall see His seed, He shall prolong His days, And the pleasure of the LORD shall prosper in His hand." **Isaiah 53:10**

Having never been separated from the Father and the Holy Spirit from eternity, Jesus experienced death, which is separation from the source of life, the Father, for the very first and last time. This He proclaimed with a loud voice on resurrection day as the Psalmist declared.

"[5] God has ascended amid shouts of joy, the LORD amid the sounding of trumpets.

[6] Sing praises to God, sing praises; sing praises to our King, sing praises. [7] For God is the King of all the earth; sing to him a psalm of praise. [8] God reigns over the nations; God is seated on his holy throne." **Psalms 47:5-8**

What did our Lord declare to the principalities, powers, rulers of the darkness, and the spiritual hosts of wickedness in the heavenly places?

"⁸ "I am the Alpha and the Omega, the Beginning and the End," says the Lord, "who is and who was and who is to come, the Almighty." **Revelation 1:8**

Then, "All authority has been given to Me in heaven and on earth." **Matthew 28:18**

This declaration to all the heavenly host brings endless joy to the holy angels but dread, defeat, and determined doom to the satanic hoards. It secures prophetic victory for the Father and the promised kingdom for the Son.

"¹ Oh, sing to the LORD a new song! For He has done marvelous things; His right hand and His holy arm have gained Him the victory. ² The LORD has made known His salvation; His righteousness He has revealed in the sight of the nations. ³ He has remembered His mercy and His faithfulness to the house of Israel; All the ends of the earth have seen the salvation of our God. ⁴ Shout joyfully to the LORD, all the earth; Break forth in song, rejoice, and sing praises. ⁵ Sing to the LORD with the harp, With the harp and the sound of a psalm, ⁶ With trumpets and the sound of a horn; Shout joyfully before the LORD, the King. ⁷ Let the sea roar, and all its fullness, The world and those who dwell in it; ⁸ Let the rivers clap their hands; Let the hills be joyful together ⁹ before the LORD, For He is coming to judge the earth. With righteousness He shall judge the world, And the peoples with equity." **Psalms 98**

"⁶ "Yet I have set My King on My holy hill of Zion." ⁷ "I will declare the decree: The LORD has said to Me, you are My Son,

Today I have begotten You. ⁸ Ask of Me, and I will give You the nations for Your inheritance, And the ends of the earth for Your possession. ⁹ You shall break them with a rod of iron; You shall dash them to pieces like a potter's vessel.'" **Psalms 2:6-9**

The resurrection also released the pledged indwelling seal of the Holy Spirit and procreated the salvation of all believers.

"¹³ In Him you also trusted, after you heard the word of truth, the gospel of your salvation; in whom also, having believed, you were sealed with the Holy Spirit of promise, ¹⁴ who is the guarantee of our inheritance until the redemption of the purchased possession, to the praise of His glory." **Ephesians 1:13-14**

"¹ Behold what manner of love the Father has bestowed on us, that we should be called children of God! Therefore, the world does not know us, because it did not know Him. ² Beloved, now we are children of God; and it has not yet been revealed what we shall be, but we know that when He is revealed, we shall be like Him, for we shall see Him as He is." **1 John 3:1-2**

"⁵⁵ "O Death, where is your sting? O Hades, where is your victory?" ⁵⁶ The sting of death is sin, and the strength of sin is the law. ⁵⁷ But thanks be to God, who gives us the victory through our Lord Jesus Christ." **1 Corinthians 15:55-57**

After the culmination of all things prophesied by the prophets, apostles, and the Lord himself, the Lord God creates a new heaven and a new earth as the first heaven and earth are dissolved. David, Isaiah, Luke, and Peter described this very event in detail. Currently, three-fourths of the earth's surface is water, but the new environment will no longer be water-based and will have completely different climatic conditions. There will be no large oceans, lakes, or seas.

"²⁵ Of old You laid the foundation of the earth, and the heavens are the work of Your hands. ²⁶ They will perish, but You will endure; Yes, they will all grow old like a garment; Like a cloak You will change them, and they will be changed." **Psalms 102:25-26**

"¹⁷ "For behold, I create new heavens and a new earth; and the former shall not be remembered or come to mind. ¹⁸ But be glad and rejoice forever in what I create; For behold, I create Jerusalem as a rejoicing, and her people a joy." **Isaiah 65:17-18**

"³³ Heaven and earth will pass away, but My words will by no means pass away." **Luke 21:33**

"¹⁰ But the day of the Lord will come as a thief in the night, in which the heavens will pass away with a great noise, and the elements will melt with fervent heat; both the earth and the works that are in it will be burned up. ¹¹ Therefore, since all these things will be dissolved, what manner of persons ought you to be in holy conduct and godliness, ¹² looking for and hastening the coming of the day of God, because of which the heavens will be dissolved, being on fire, and the elements will melt with fervent heat? ¹³ Nevertheless we, according to His promise, look for new heavens and a new earth in which righteousness dwells." **2 Peter 3:10-13**

"¹ Now I saw a new heaven and a new earth, for the first heaven and the first earth had passed away. Also, there was no more sea." **Revelation 21:1**

Not only are the heavens and earth recreated, the earthly abode of the saints, the residence that Jesus promised to prepare for the church, is also ready for her occupants. By this point in the concatenation of Revelation, Old Testament saints, tribulation saints, and all those converted during the millennial kingdom will be assimilated into the redeemed bride and will dwell in the New Jerusalem. Only the people born in natural bodies during the millennial kingdom will dwell on the earth. The apostle Paul described the consummation of all things in Christ, while the apostle John described the New Jerusalem descending into the eternal age.

"^{28} Now when all things are made subject to Him, then the Son Himself will also be subject to Him who put all things under Him, that God may be all in all." **1 Corinthians 15:28**

"^{2} Then I, John, saw the holy city, New Jerusalem, coming down out of heaven from God, prepared as a bride adorned for her husband." **Revelation 21:2**

This eternal earthly abode of the saints concludes with the original plan of God being fulfilled—the Lord God tabernacling with men and dwelling with us in the midst of the New Jerusalem. Sin will never rear its ugly head again, and it will never be possible for anyone to commit sin again because everyone there will be in love with the Lord.

"^{3} And I heard a loud voice from heaven saying, "Behold, the tabernacle of God is with men, and He will dwell with them, and they shall be His people. God Himself will be with them and be their God. ^{4} And God will wipe away every tear from their eyes; there shall be no more death, nor sorrow, nor crying. There shall be no more pain, for the former things have passed away." **Revelation 21:3-4**

This new city will be the highest point on all the earth, possibly seen from every corner of the earth. The New Jerusalem takes on the character of its inhabitants, the Most High God in all of His glory and the redeemed beloved saints from the history of all mankind.

"¹⁰And he carried me away in the Spirit to a mountain great and high, and showed me the Holy City, Jerusalem, coming down out of heaven from God. ¹¹ It shone with the glory of God, and its brilliance was like that of a very precious jewel, like a jasper, clear as crystal. ¹² It had a great, high wall with twelve gates, and with twelve angels at the gates. On the gates were written the names of the twelve tribes of Israel. ¹³ There were three gates on the east, three on the north, three on the south and three on the west. ¹⁴ The wall of the city had twelve foundations, and on them were the names of the twelve apostles of the Lamb…²² I did not see a temple in the city, because the Lord God Almighty and the Lamb are its temple. ²³ The city does not need the sun or the moon to shine on it, for the glory of God gives it light, and the Lamb is its lamp." **Revelation 21:10-14, 22-23**

With billions of occupants, the city must be gargantuan. The dimensions of the city and the walls surrounding the city are provided by the apostle John. What a beautiful site she is! This beloved is the true emerald city.

"¹⁵ The angel who talked with me had a measuring rod of gold to measure the city, its gates and its walls. ¹⁶ The city was laid out like a square, as long as it was wide. He measured the city with the rod and found it to be 12,000 stadia in length, and as wide and high as it is long. ¹⁷ The angel measured the wall using human measurement, and it was 144 cubits thick. ¹⁸ The wall was made of jasper, and the city of pure gold, as pure as glass. ¹⁹ The foundations of the city walls were decorated with every kind of precious stone. The first foundation was jasper, the second sapphire, the third agate, the fourth emerald, [20] the fifth onyx, the sixth ruby, the seventh chrysolite, the eighth beryl, the ninth topaz, the tenth turquoise, the eleventh jacinth, and the twelfth amethyst. [21] The twelve gates were twelve pearls, each gate made of a single pearl. The great street of the city was of gold, as pure as transparent glass." **Revelation 21:15-21**

The city will not require electricity or the light from the sun as it will never be night there. Isn't that wonderful, beloved! We will not need to eat, sleep, or rest throughout eternity. The interior will be like the Garden of Eden with the river of the water of life flowing from the throne of the Holiest of All, and the tree of life will line the streets.

"[1] Then the angel showed me the river of the water of life, as clear as crystal, flowing from the throne of God and of the Lamb [2] down the middle of the great street of the city. On each side of the river stood the tree of life, bearing twelve crops of fruit, yielding its fruit every month. And the leaves of the tree are for the healing of the nations. [3] No longer will there be any curse. The throne of God and of the Lamb will be in the city, and his servants will serve him. [4] They will see his face, and his name will be on their foreheads. [5] There will be no more night. They will not need the light of a lamp or the light of the sun, for the Lord God will give them light. And they will reign for ever and ever." **Revelation 22:1-5**

As I communicate the particulars of the New Jerusalem as it is written in the word of God to all my brothers and sisters in Christ, I can hardly contain my exuberance to reach my eternal home.

How long, O Lord, faithful and true, must I wait to see Your glorious face and to humbly bow before the majestic throne of glory to worship You, my Lord, my God, my Savior, and King. O Father, how I long to come home to be with You. Nevertheless, Holy Father, not my will but Yours be done.

"^{12} "Behold, I am coming soon! My reward is with me, and I will give to each person according to what they have done. ^{13} I am the Alpha and the Omega, the First and the Last, the Beginning and the End. ^{14} "Blessed are those who wash their robes, that they may have the right to the tree of life and may go through the gates into the city. ^{15} Outside are the dogs, those who practice magic arts, the sexually immoral, the murderers, the idolaters and everyone who loves and practices falsehood. ^{16} "I, Jesus, have sent my angel to give you this testimony for the churches. I am the Root and the Offspring of David, and the bright Morning Star."

^{17} The Spirit and the bride say, "Come!" And let the one who hears say, "Come!" Let the one who is thirsty come; and let the one who wishes take the free gift of the water of life." **Revelation 22:12-17**

PART 2

THE SEEKER
OF LOST SHEEP

CHAPTER 1

SHEEP AND GOATS

Below is a list of key secondary principles. Obviously, there may be others that can easily be added, but if these are applied, one will be on a solid foundation.

- Read the entire Bible, Old and New Testaments—remember, Revelation is a culmination of the other 65 books of the Bible.
- Never reassign messages that are meant for Israel and/or the Church. They are not the same entities. The Church does not replace Israel. Israel is the Father's wife, and the Church is the Son's bride.
- The Bible is the best commentator on the Bible.
- Never lift a verse out of its context—remember, a verse without context is a pretext.
- The world only has two classes of people—believers and unbelievers.
- Always apply all of God's attributes equally—God's love does not void God's holiness; God's mercy does not void God's righteousness.

- Never intermingle the free gift of salvation and works (a Christian's lifestyle after salvation). Grace is a gift to be received, imputed righteousness by faith in the death, burial, and resurrection of Christ. On the other hand, through the indwelling Holy Spirit, works are the empowerment of behavior, activities, intent, and motives that will be rewarded only if these acts are pure, that is to say, completely performed by the Holy Spirit through the believer.

One of the most important principles listed above is to know and understand that all people currently alive in this world are divided into two groups and only two groups: believers and unbelievers, that is it. There are other ways to say such as sheep and goats, wheat and tares, saved and lost, children and dogs, possessors and pretenders, twice-born and once-born, alive and dead. No matter what description one gives, the fact remains that the people of the world are divided into two groups.

Jesus said it this way, "[18]he that believeth on the Son is not condemned but he that believeth not is condemned already." **John 3:18**

You may ask: Why would unbelievers already be condemned?

Well Jesus provides the only answer to this question, "[19]because he hath not believed in the name of the only begotten Son of God." **John 3:19**

That is it, my friend. Notice that Jesus did not mention anything about one's behavior.

You may ask: Why not?

Because only the Son of God, the Lord Jesus Christ, can please the Father. Everyone who goes to heaven possesses two things, the love of God and eternal life. This is how believers can have absolute assurance that their salvation is eternally secure.

1. The love of God is only located in one place:
    a. "^{39}nothing…shall be able to separate us from the love of God **which is in Christ Jesus our Lord." Rom. 8:39**
2. Eternal life is a person:
    a. "^{10}Whoever believes in the Son of God accepts this testimony. Whoever does not believe God has made him out to be a liar, because they have not believed the testimony God has given about his Son. ^{11} And this is the testimony: **God has given us eternal life**, (where is this life located) and **this life is in his Son**. ^{12} **Whoever has the Son has life**; whoever does not have the Son of God does not have life." **1 John 5:10-12**
    b. "^{18}**We know** that anyone born of God does not continue to sin; **the One (Jesus) who was born of God keeps them safe**, and the evil one cannot harm them. ^{19} **We know** that we are children of God, and that the whole world is under the control of the evil one. ^{20} **We know** also that the Son of God has come and has given us understanding, so that we may know him who is true. And **we are in him** who is true **by being in his Son Jesus Christ. He (Jesus) is the true God and eternal life." 1 John 5:18-20**

How glorious is that! **We know** we have eternal life because **Jesus lives inside of us** in the person of the Holy Spirit! All glory, honor, and praise be unto You, O Lord God, holy, righteous, just, and true. For You are full of compassion, slow to anger, and of plenteous mercy. Your holy arm and Your righteous right hand have gotten You the victory. Thank You for predestinating, calling, justifying, and glorifying all those who have placed their trust in You.

"³³Who will bring any charge against those whom God has chosen? It is God who justifies. ³⁴ Who then is the one who condemns? No one. Christ Jesus, who died more than that, who was raised to life is at the right hand of God and is also interceding for us. ³⁵ Who shall separate us from the love of Christ? Shall trouble or hardship or persecution or famine or nakedness or danger or sword? ³⁶ As it is written: "For your sake we face death all day long; we are considered as sheep to be slaughtered." ³⁷ No, in all these things we are more than conquerors through him who loved us. ³⁸ For I am convinced that neither death nor life, neither angels nor demons, neither the present nor the future, nor any powers, ³⁹ neither height nor depth, nor anything else in all creation, will be able to separate us from the love of God that is in Christ Jesus our Lord. **Rom. 8:33-39**

"⁵¹ Listen, I tell you a mystery: We will not all sleep, but we will all be changed ⁵² in a flash, in the twinkling of an eye, at the last trumpet. For the trumpet will sound, the dead will be raised imperishable, and we will be changed. ⁵³ For the perishable must clothe itself with the imperishable, and the mortal with immortality. ⁵⁴ When the perishable has been clothed with the imperishable, and the mortal with immortality, then the saying that is written will come true: "Death has been swallowed up in victory." ⁵⁵ "Where, O death, is your victory? Where, O death, is your sting?" ⁵⁶ The sting of death is sin, and the power of sin is the law. ⁵⁷ But thanks be to God! He gives us the victory through our Lord Jesus Christ. ⁵⁸ Therefore, my dear brothers and sisters, stand firm. Let nothing move you. Always give yourselves fully to the work of the Lord because you know that your labor in the Lord is not in vain. **1 Corinthians 15:51-58**

Oh, dear friend, please listen to me. How religious, nice, intelligent, courageous, or any other behavior traits people think would help them get to heaven do not matter.

You ask: Why not?

Because we are born into the devil's kingdom, and good behavior cannot transfer us into God's kingdom.

"[10]For it is with your heart that you believe and are justified, and it is with your mouth that you profess your faith and are saved." **Rom. 10:10**

The writer of Proverbs states it this way, "Above all else, guard your heart, for everything you do flows from it. **Prov. 4:23**

"[7] For as he thinks in his heart, so is he…" **Prov. 23:7**

You see, true belief starts from the inside of a person then is revealed or manifested in their behavior and speech. A true conversion internally will always produce true change in behavior externally. It is called a metamorphosis, like a caterpillar turning into a beautiful butterfly. Jesus comes in and cleans up our behavior through conviction, correction, and chastisement of the Holy Spirit. We are powerless to do that.

Now, let us define the two terms:

Believers—those who have confessed to God that they are lost sinners and have received Christ as Lord and Savior. All their sins, past, present, and future, have been transferred from their account onto Jesus' upon the cross and three days in the grave.

The proof that God has accepted Christ's substitutionary sacrifice is the bodily resurrection of His Son, Jesus, from the grave and seating him upon the throne in heaven, thereby giving Jesus all authority in heaven and earth. God treated Jesus as if he committed the believer's sins. The eternal wrath of God was poured out on the eternal Son of God on the cross. The righteousness of Jesus was transferred to the believer. In God's eyes, the believer is now washed, blameless, and holy only because of Jesus. It has absolutely nothing to do with service (good works) as righteousness is imputed (credited) to the believer.

Unbelievers—those who have not confessed to God that they are lost sinners and have not received Christ as Lord and Savior. All their sins remain with them, and the eternal wrath of God is upon those sins, therefore upon the sinner. They possess their own righteousness, which, when compared to Jesus' righteousness, is declared by God as unrighteousness.

"²Although some may be religious or have a zeal for God, it is not according to true knowledge. For they, being ignorant of God's righteousness, are going about to establish their own righteousness, and have not submitted themselves unto the righteousness of God." **Romans 10:2-3**

They do not understand that the eternal God requires an eternal blood sacrifice to satisfy his eternal wrath upon sin. Only Jesus, the eternal Son of God, offered up by the eternal Holy Spirit, was able to accomplish that for all sinners.

"¹⁴How much more, then, will the blood of Christ, who through the eternal Spirit offered himself unblemished to God, cleanse our consciences from acts that lead to death, so that we may serve the living God!" **Hebrews 9:14**

One world, two groups. God is Father to believers and is Judge to unbelievers. God's interaction with each group is 180 degrees apart. From the Lord's perspective, the believers are under grace and are treated as children. Unbelievers are under wrath and are treated as enemies at war against God.

You may say: Now wait a minute, I am not an enemy of God, and I'm definitely not at war with God! Well, my friend, you may not be an enemy and at war with God, but God said that He's your enemy and is at war with you. He has also declared that you are currently and will forever be under the wrath of God if you remain an unbeliever.

"³⁶He that believeth on the Son hath everlasting life: and he that believeth not hath not life **but the wrath of God abides on him**." **John 3:36**

That word abide means that the wrath of God is currently on the unbeliever and will forever continue until one believes during their lifetime on earth.

In **Col. 3:5-6,** Paul calls the unbelievers the children of disobedience and stated, "⁵ Therefore put to death your members which are on the earth: fornication, uncleanness, passion, evil desire, and covetousness, which is idolatry. ⁶ **Because of these things the wrath of God is coming upon the sons of disobedience**,"

The phrase "is coming" means continues.

"³ But fornication and all uncleanness or covetousness, let it not even be named among you, as is fitting for saints; ⁴ neither filthiness, nor foolish talking, nor coarse jesting, which are not fitting, but rather giving of thanks. ⁵ For this you know, that no fornicator, unclean person, nor covetous man, who is an idolater, has any inheritance in the kingdom of Christ and God. ⁶ Let no one deceive you with empty words, for because of these things **the wrath of God comes upon the sons of disobedience.** ⁷ Therefore do not be partakers with them." **Ephesians 5:3-7**

"¹⁸ **The wrath of God** is being revealed from heaven **against all the godlessness and wickedness of people, who suppress the truth by their wickedness,** ¹⁹ since what may be known about God is plain to them, because God has made it plain to them. ²⁰ For since the creation of the world God's invisible qualities his eternal power and divine nature have been clearly seen, being understood from what has been made, so that **people are without excuse**. ²¹ For although they knew God, they neither glorified him as God nor gave thanks to him, but their thinking became futile, and their foolish hearts were darkened. ²² Although they claimed to be wise, they became fools." **Rom. 1:18-22**

"⁵But because of your stubbornness and your unrepentant heart, you are **storing up wrath against yourself for the day of God's wrath**, when his righteous judgment will be revealed. God "will repay each person according to what they have done." ...**for those who are self-seeking and who reject the truth and follow evil, there will be wrath and anger.**" **Rom. 2:5-8**

"¹⁴ Blessed are those who do His commandments, that they may have the right to the tree of life and may enter through the gates into the city. ¹⁵ But outside (of heaven) are dogs and sorcerers and sexually immoral and murderers and idolaters, and whoever loves and practices a lie." **Revelation 22:14-15**

Dogs, sorcerers, sexually immoral, murderers, idolaters, and liars are all descriptions given by God of unbelievers. Friend, there is a day of reckoning coming! God's wrath grows daily with the daily sins committed by the unbeliever.

"¹¹God judges (sustains) the righteous and, **God is angry with the wicked (unbeliever) every day.**" **Psalms 7:11**

"⁶Seeing it is a righteous thing with God to recompense tribulation to them that trouble you; and to you who are troubled rest with us, when the Lord Jesus shall be revealed from heaven with his mighty angels, **in flaming fire taking vengeance on them that do not know God and do not obey the gospel of our Lord Jesus Christ. Who shall be punished with everlasting destruction from the presence of the Lord, and the glory of his power**; when he shall come to be glorified in saints and to be admired in all them that believe (because our testimony among you was believed) in that day." **II Thessalonians 1:6-8**

This text points out the true nature of the unbeliever. They do not know God, and they do not obey God.

I can continue, but you get the point.

CHAPTER 2

LOST AND FOUND

So, how does God deal with one of his children who goes astray? Most, if not all, of us have heard or read the story of the prodigal son. For those that have not, it is found in the book of Luke.

"[11] Jesus continued: "There was a man who had two sons. [12] The younger one said to his father, 'Father, give me my share of the estate.' So he divided his property between them. [13] "Not long after that, the younger son got together all he had, set off for a distant country and there squandered his wealth in wild living. [14] After he had spent everything, there was a severe famine in that whole country, and he began to be in need. [15] So he went and hired himself out to a citizen of that country, who sent him to his fields to feed pigs. [16] He longed to fill his stomach with the pods that the pigs were eating, but no one gave him anything. [17] "When he came to his senses, he said, 'How many of my father's hired servants have food to spare, and here I am starving to death! [18] I will set out and go back to my father and say to him: Father, I have sinned against heaven and against you. [19] I am no longer worthy to be called your son; make me like one of your hired servants.' [20] So he got up and went to his father. "But while he was still a long way off, his father saw him and was filled with compassion for him; he ran to his son, threw his arms around him and kissed him. ²¹ "The son said to him, 'Father, I have sinned against heaven and against you. I am no longer worthy to be called your son.' ²² "But the father said to his servants, 'Quick! Bring the best robe and put it on him. Put a ring on his finger and sandals on his feet. ²³ Bring the fattened calf and kill it. Let's have a feast and celebrate. ²⁴ For this son of mine was dead and is alive again; he was lost and is found.' So they began to celebrate. ²⁵ "Meanwhile, the older son was in the field. When he came near the house, he heard music and dancing. ²⁶ So he called one of the servants and asked him what was going on. ²⁷ 'Your brother has come,' he replied, 'and your father has killed the fattened calf because he has him back safe and sound.' ²⁸ "The older brother became angry and refused to go in. So his father went out and pleaded with him. ²⁹ But he answered his father, 'Look! All these years I've been slaving for you and never disobeyed your orders. Yet you never gave me even a young goat so I could celebrate with my friends. ³⁰ But when this son of yours who has squandered your property with prostitutes comes home, you kill the fattened calf for him!' ³¹ "'My son,' the father said, 'you are always with me, and everything I have is yours. ³² But we had to celebrate and be glad, because this brother of yours was dead and is alive again; he was lost and is found.'" **Luke 15:11-32**

This story was presented to us by the Lord Jesus, and we all understand the meaning that a wayward son is still a son not a pig, but his inheritance is no more.

What is meant by "his inheritance is no more"?

Didn't Peter declare that God has "³…given us new birth into a living hope through the resurrection of Jesus Christ from the dead, ⁴and into **an inheritance that can never perish, spoil or fade.**"? **1 Peter 1:3-4**

Yes. However, Peter was speaking of the house the Lord went away to prepare for us, our room in the Father's house.

"¹Do not let your hearts be troubled. You believe in God; believe also in me. ² My Father's house has many rooms; if that were not so, would I have told you that I am going there to prepare a place for you? ³ And if I go and prepare a place for you, I will come back and take you to be with me that you also may be where I am." **John 14:1-3**

That inheritance is for every member of the Church (the true body of believers) and is solely based on positional salvation imputed to us by faith in Christ. It is something we receive as a heavenly birthright, or to say it in earthly terms, regenerated believers are born with a golden spoon in their mouths. The day you are born-again, you received the reservation from the Father through the Son, and it is sealed by the Holy Spirit. It takes the work of the entire Godhead to secure our salvation.

The inheritance that I am speaking of is not salvation and is not gained by heavenly birthright, it is awarded by the Lord Jesus at the judgment seat of Christ based on the believer's lifestyle **after** being born again into the kingdom of Christ.

"²² Now that **you have purified yourselves** by obeying the truth so that you have sincere love for each other, love one another deeply, from the heart. ²³ For **you have been born again**, not of perishable seed, but of imperishable, through the living and enduring word of God." **1 Pet. 1:22-23**

"¹ See what great love the Father has lavished on us, that we should be called children of God! And that is what we are! The reason the world does not know us is that it did not know him. ² Dear friends, now we are children of God, and what we will be has not yet been made known. But we know that when Christ appears, we shall be like him, for we shall see him as he is. ³ **All who have this hope in him purify themselves, just as he is pure." 1 John 3:1-3**

The objective here is not to discuss eternal security, which all true believers have, but to focus on how the Lord responds to his children who misbehave, that is, commit sins.

CHAPTER 3

FROM CORRUPTION TO GLORY

Let us take a brief moment to address a severe misconception among believers. The popular views on sinning believers are:

1. They were never saved.
2. They lose their salvation and must repent to regain it.
3. It does not matter how they live after salvation because they are eternally secure.

All three views, although popular, are not biblical. The truth is that all believers sin every day, all day. That is why we continually require a Savior.

You may say: Wait one minute. What do you mean by sin all day?

Let me put you in remembrance, and please never forget, "²³all have sinned and **come short of God's glory**" **Rom. 3:23**

Please do not overlook the last segment of that scriptural verse, as it is the key to understanding the grace required to save us. If you doubt that all believers sin all day, then let me, well, not me but God, ask you a few questions.

"⁷Brace yourself like a man; I (the LORD GOD) will question you, and you shall answer me.

1. ⁸ "Would you discredit my justice?
2. Would you condemn me to justify yourself?
3. ⁹ Do you have an arm like God's?
4. And can your voice thunder like his?

Well, can you?

5. ¹⁰ Then adorn yourself with glory and splendor,
6. And clothe yourself in honor and majesty.
7. ¹¹ Unleash the fury of your wrath, look at all who are proud and bring them low,
8. ¹² look at all who are proud and humble them,
9. Crush the wicked where they stand.
10. ¹³ Bury them all in the dust together;
11. shroud their faces in the grave (hell).

If you can do all these things:

"¹⁴ Then I myself (the LORD GOD) will admit to you that your own right hand can save you (keep you saved)." **Job 40:7-14**

Allow me to place you in remembrance of the topic of our discussion. "²³all have sinned and **come short of God's glory**" **Rom. 3:23**

Now Beloved, let me show you what the glory of the Lord looks like.

"¹⁶Then it came to pass on the third day, in the morning, that there were thunderings and lightnings, and a thick cloud on the mountain;

and the sound of the trumpet was very loud, so that all the people who were in the camp trembled. [17] And Moses brought the people out of the camp to meet with God, and they stood at the foot of the mountain. [18] Now Mount Sinai was completely in smoke, because the LORD descended upon it in fire. Its smoke ascended like the smoke of a furnace, and the whole mountain quaked greatly. [19] And when the blast of the trumpet sounded long and became louder and louder, Moses spoke, and God answered him by voice." **Exodus 19:16-19**

Do the mountains tremble in your presence? Does everything within the vicinity become engulfed with fire from the glory of your presence?

"[16] And the glory of the LORD abode upon mount Sinai, and the cloud covered it six days: and the seventh day he called unto Moses out of the midst of the cloud. [17] And the sight of the glory of the LORD was like devouring fire on the top of the mount in the eyes of the children of Israel." **Exodus 24:16-17**

Our God is holy. Our God is eternally, perfectly, gloriously, majestically holy. He requires perfection in holiness from eternity to eternity. Have you ever done anything perfect? Are your prayers perfect? Is your service perfectly holy? Are you from everlasting to everlasting?

If you are not eternally, perfectly, gloriously, majestically holy, if you cannot do the eleven things listed above, Mr., Mrs., sir, and madam believer, you still need a Savior. Jesus is eternal, and all these things happen in Jesus' presence. That is why He alone can save and keep us saved.

You and I still come short of God's glory. Though the record of our sins is erased upon the cross, buried in the tomb, and we have new life through the resurrection, we are not yet perfected. "¹ Behold what great love the Father has lavished on us, that we should be called children of God! And that is what we are! The reason the world does not know us is that it did not know him. ² Dear friends, now we are children of God, and what we will be has not yet been made known. **But we know that when Christ appears, we shall be like him, for we shall see him as he is.** ³ All who have this hope in him purify themselves, just as he is pure." **1 John 3:1-3**

So, what does Jesus look like today? ⁸ "I am the Alpha and the Omega," says the Lord God, "who is, and who was, and who is to come, the Almighty."…" ¹² I (John) turned around to see the voice that was speaking to me. And when I turned I saw seven golden lampstands, ¹³ and among the lampstands was someone like a son of man, **dressed in a robe reaching down to his feet** and with **a golden sash around his chest**. ¹⁴ The **hair on his head was white like wool, as white as snow, and his eyes were like blazing fire**. ¹⁵ His **feet were like bronze glowing in a furnace**, and his **voice was like the sound of rushing waters**. ¹⁶ In his right hand he held seven stars, and **coming out of his mouth was a sharp, double-edged sword**. His **face was like the sun shining in all its brilliance**." **Revelation 1:8, 12-16**

"²⁶Above the vault over their heads was what looked like a throne of lapis lazuli, and high above on the throne was a figure like that of a man. ²⁷ I saw that from what appeared to be **his waist up he looked like glowing metal, as if full of fire**, and that **from there down he looked like fire; and brilliant light surrounded him**. ²⁸ Like the appearance of a rainbow in the clouds on a rainy day, **so was the radiance around him**. This was the appearance of the likeness of the glory of the LORD." **Ezk. 1:26-28**

"⁵ I looked up and there before me was a man **dressed in linen, with a belt of fine gold from Uphaz around his waist.** ⁶ **His body was like topaz, his face like lightning, his eyes like flaming torches, his arms and legs like the gleam of burnished bronze, and his voice like the sound of a multitude.**" **Dan. 10:5-6**

How will you and I react if we saw Jesus today? Just like John, "¹⁷ When I saw him, I fell at his feet as though dead." **Revelation 1:17**

Ezekiel, "²⁸When I saw it, I fell facedown" **Ezk. 1:28**

And Daniel, "⁷ I, Daniel, was the only one who saw the vision; those who were with me did not see it, but such terror overwhelmed them that they fled and hid themselves. ⁸ So I was left alone, gazing at this great vision; I had no strength left, my face turned deathly pale and I was helpless. ⁹ Then I heard him speaking, and as I listened to him, I fell into a deep sleep, my face to the ground." **Dan. 10:7-9**

Oh, beloved, do you not understand? He is holy! We cannot just walk into His presence. He is holy! Our God is holy.

What did Jesus say about the believer's works? "⁷And which of you, having a servant plowing or tending sheep, will say to him when he has come in from the field, 'Come at once and sit down to eat'? ⁸ But will he not rather say to him, 'Prepare something for my supper, and gird yourself and serve me till I have eaten and drunk, and afterward you will eat and drink'? ⁹ **Does he thank that servant because he did the things that were commanded him? I THINK NOT.** ¹⁰ So likewise you, when you have done all those things which you are commanded, say, 'We

are unprofitable servants. We have done what was our duty to do.'" Luke 17:7-10

Then what are we to do? "¹¹ But you, O man (believer) of God, flee *evil* things and pursue righteousness, godliness, faith, love, patience, gentleness. ¹² Fight the good fight of faith, lay hold on eternal life (Jesus), to which you were also called and have confessed the good confession in the presence of many witnesses. ¹³ I urge you in the sight of God who gives life to all things, and before Christ Jesus who witnessed the good confession before Pontius Pilate, ¹⁴ that you keep this commandment without spot, blameless until our Lord Jesus Christ's appearing, ¹⁵ which He will manifest in His own time, He who is the blessed and only Potentate (Sovereign), the King of kings and Lord of lords, ¹⁶ who alone has immortality, **dwelling in unapproachable light**, whom no man has seen or can see, to whom be honor and everlasting power. Amen." **1 Tim 6:11-16**

Since we are living here upon the earth in our unredeemable mortal body, called the flesh, there is nothing we can do that is not contaminated by the flesh. Believers' inner man (our spirit) are washed and regenerated by the Holy Spirit.

"But when the kindness and love of God our Savior appeared, ⁵ he saved us, **not because of righteous things we had done**, but because of his mercy. He saved us **through the washing of rebirth and renewal by the Holy Spirit**, ⁶ whom he poured out on us generously through Jesus Christ our Savior, ⁷ so that, having been justified by his grace, we might become heirs having the hope of eternal life." **Titus 3:4-7**

Nevertheless, the Holy Spirit places the desire within us and provides the power unto us to obey God.

"…for it is God (the Holy Spirit) who works in you to will (set desire) and to act (empower) in order to fulfill his good purpose."
Philippians 2:13

Therefore, we cannot take credit for any good behaviors pleasing to God because it is God himself doing the works. Yet, in His loving kindness, He rewards us for being a yielded vessel through whom He can distribute blessings and declaration of the gospel.

PART 3

FROM MILK TO MEAT

CHAPTER 1

THE PERFECT CANDIDATE FOR SALVATION

During His earthly ministry, Jesus persistently invited unbelieving Jews to salvation perfection, which came only through faith and by following Him. In the third and final year of His ministry, as He departed Galilee, which is in northern Israel, Jesus traveled south into the region of Judea. He and the disciples traveled beyond the Jordon River near Jerusalem, where great multitudes followed Him, and He performed many miracles. Immediately upon His return to the region, the usual antagonistic suspects arrived attempting to ensnare Jesus with their questions. They enquired about marriage and divorce, as it was taught by the Rabbis during those days that a man can divorce his wife for any reason. However, Jesus made it clear that they errored in their interpretation of the scriptures, as marriage was a picture of the faithfulness between Christ and His bride, whom He would never divorce.

Then He turned His attention to the little children who were brought unto Him for blessings, which He cheerfully did. Somewhere in the background, watching all these things, was a rich young ruler who was the perfect candidate for salvation.

"²¹ Jesus said to him, "If you want to be perfect, go, sell what you have and give to the poor, and you will have treasure in heaven; and come, follow Me." **Matthew 19:21**

Here is a rhetorical question. What would make the rich young ruler perfect, his works of selling his possessions and giving his proceeds to the poor or following Jesus? Does perfect here mean maturity? Of course not. Jesus is talking about salvation. This young man was keeping the law as best he could. Perfect? No, but as best he could.

"¹⁶ Now behold, one came and said to Him, "Good Teacher, what good thing shall I do that I may have eternal life?" ¹⁷ So He said to him, "Why do you call Me good? No one is good but One; that is, God. But if you want to enter into life, keep the commandments." ¹⁸ He said to Him, "Which ones?" Jesus said, "'You shall not murder,' 'You shall not commit adultery,' 'You shall not steal,' 'You shall not bear false witness,' ¹⁹ Honor your father and your mother,' and, you shall love your neighbor as yourself.'" ²⁰ The young man said to Him, "All these things I have kept from my youth. **What do I still lack?**" ²¹ Jesus said to him, "If you want to be perfect, go, sell what you have and give to the poor, and you will have treasure in heaven; and come, follow Me." ²² But when the young man heard that saying, he went away sorrowful, for he had great possessions." **Matthew 19:16-22**

Let us dissect the conversation. We know who Jesus is, but who is this rich young ruler, why would he seek out Jesus, and why this specific question?

The first things we note about this man was that he was young and a ruler. Matthew said he was young. Luke said that he was a ruler.

"¹⁸ Now a certain ruler asked Him, saying," **Luke 18:18**

The fact that Luke stated that the young man is a ruler, does that mean anything to you? Well, it did to the Jews living under the law in that day. Listen to what the law says about how you were to address a ruler.

"²⁸ "You shall not revile God, nor curse a ruler of your people." Exodus 22:28

The Greek word used in Luke 18:18 for the word ruler is "archon," meaning chief, magistrate, prince. This was quite a position for a young man during those days, more than likely the leader of the local synagogue and a member of the Pharisees.

Why a Pharisee?

Because he believed in life after death and the Sadducees did not.

"¹⁷ Now as He was going out on the road, one came running, knelt before Him, and asked Him," **Mark 10:17**

Second, he came running to Jesus, which clearly indicated an urgency. He did not want to miss the opportunity to resolve the question in his mind, which was: Am I saved? The Jews believed, and the Old Testament teaches for Israel that heaven will be here on earth in the Kingdom of the Messiah. He wanted to know if he was doing well enough to make it into the Kingdom. Recognizing that Jesus could answer this question because he had not only heard about Jesus but most likely listened to one or more of the Lord's sermons and perhaps was witness to several of the miracles performed by the Lord, thereby convincing the young man that if anyone knew the answer to this longing question in his heart, it would be Jesus. This illustrates the futility of religion.

It can never satisfy nor provide absolute assurance of salvation. Only Christ can.

Third, he knelt at the feet of Jesus. Do you know the significance of this act? For a ruler of the Jews to openly acknowledge that Jesus was his superior shows that he was seeking assurance that the path he was on was the straight and narrow road.

Fourth, the formal acknowledgment, "Good Teacher." This is amazing yet perhaps understandable since this was a young man, that someone skilled in the scriptures would ever call another human "good." The Old Testament makes it clear that there is no such thing as a good human in the eyes of the Lord.

"[1] The fool has said in his heart, "There is no God." They are corrupt, they have done abominable works, there is none who does good. [2] The LORD looks down from heaven upon the children of men, to see if there are any who understand, who seek God. [3] They have all turned aside, they have together become corrupt; There is none who does good, No, not one.[4] Have all the workers of iniquity no knowledge, who eat up my people as they eat bread, And do not call on the LORD?" **Psalms 14:1-4**

These same verses are repeated verbatim in **Psalms 53:1-4**. One would expect a ruler or leader of a synagogue to know this, but it was obvious that they had no knowledge, nor was there any understanding of the scriptures. The first thing the Lord does is correct his theology, then forces him to make a decision, stating, "Why do you call Me good? No one is good but One, that is, God." **Mark 10:18**

He had to decide if Jesus is who he claims to be, the Son of God, Messiah the Prince. There is only one way Jesus could be a "Good

Teacher," he had to be God. If, in fact, Jesus is God, the Jewish Messiah, then the young man, being a Jew, would be obligated to obey, without reservation, the words of Jesus.

The Lord goes straight to the heart of the young ruler's problem to reveal the two essential elements that will keep numerous people from entering the kingdom of heaven.

1. Relationships
    a. Toward God— "^{37} Jesus said to him, '"You shall love the LORD your God with all your heart, with all your soul, and with all your mind.' ^{38} This is the first and great commandment." **Matthew 22:37-38** The young man failed this test when he refused to acknowledge the Messiahship claim of Jesus; therefore, there was no need to state commandments 1 through 4.

"^{39} You search the Scriptures, for in them you think you have eternal life; and these are they which testify of Me. ^{40} But you are not willing to come to Me that you may have life." **John 5:39-40**

You say: How do you know he rejects Jesus' claim to be the Messiah?

Well, let us read his answer to the Lord.

"Teacher, all these things I have kept from my youth." **Mark 10:20**

Did you notice that he omitted "Good" from his response? He understood what Jesus was saying. Jesus traveled all Israel claiming to be the Messiah by signs and wonders as well as His words. He knelt at Jesus' feet nonetheless. When challenged to make a decision concerning the person of Jesus, the young man rejected Jesus' claim, unlike the disciples.

> b. Toward people— "³⁹ And the second is like it: 'You shall love your neighbor as yourself.' ⁴⁰ On these two commandments hang all the Law and the Prophets." **Matthew 22:39-40**

The Lord said to the young ruler, "¹⁹ You know the commandments: 'Do not commit adultery,' 'Do not murder,' 'Do not steal,' 'Do not bear false witness,' 'Do not defraud,' 'Honor your father and your mother.'" **Mark 10:19**

In my mind's eye, I can envision the young man bubbling with excitement over Jesus' response as he eagerly proclaimed, most likely, loudly, that he has kept the commandments from his youth.

You may ask: You don't believe him?

Well, it is not that I do not believe him. The word of God declares that no one can keep them. We must remember that the commandments require perfection in perfect holiness equal to God's perfection and holiness. So, no, I do not believe him nor anyone else who may make such a claim.

"¹⁹ Now we know that whatever the law says, it says to those who are under the law, that every mouth may be stopped, and all the world may become guilty before God. ²⁰ Therefore by the deeds of the law no flesh will be justified in His sight, for by the law is the knowledge of sin." **Romans 3:19-20**

Please pay close attention to the Lord's response to this young man. He could have laughed in his face and told him about every time he disobeyed each one of those commandments, but instead, the Lord had compassion. Listen to this:

"²¹ Then Jesus, looking at him, loved him, and said to him, "One thing you lack: Go your way, sell whatever you have and give to the poor, and you will have treasure in heaven; and come, take up the cross, and follow Me." **Mark 10:21**

Jesus looked upon this lost sheep and loved him even while the rich young ruler was enslaved within his religious piety. How glorious is the mercy and compassion of our God.

Jesus pointed him to the one thing that can fill the void in his life and bring complete peace, tranquility, hope, and assurance. Believe in Me. Change your mind about Me. Believe Me when I tell you that I am the Good Teacher, the Messiah, the Son of God. Leave your religion and pledge your allegiance to Me and obey Me. Jesus was not making either philanthropy or destitution a requirement for salvation because neither is. However, what the Lord did was expose the young man's heart. He was not blameless, as he asserted since he loved his possessions more than his neighbors. Of greater importance, he refused to obey the Lord's direct command, give up the temporary earthly riches and I will give you eternal treasures in heaven. The young man chose to serve earthly riches instead of God.

"²⁴ "No one can serve two masters; for either he will hate the one and love the other, or else he will be loyal to the one and despise the other. You cannot serve God and mammon." **Matthew 6:24**

What Jesus was attempting to do with the young ruler was to have him determine whether he would submit to the Lordship of Christ no matter what Jesus asked of him. Hence, as he would not in any way acknowledge his own sinful condition and repent, neither would he submit to the Sovereign Savior. Such unwillingness on both counts is what kept him from the eternal life he so eagerly sought.

"³⁴ When He had called the people to Himself, with His disciples also, He said to them, "Whoever desires to come after Me, let him deny himself, and take up his cross, and follow Me. ³⁵ For whoever desires to save his life will lose it, but whoever loses his life for My sake and the gospel's will save it." **Mark 8:34-35**

What did the young ruler turn down for the temporary satisfaction of earthly goods? He gave up eternal treasure in heaven that will never fade away. Salvation and all its benefits, given by the Father who dwells in heaven, both in this life and the life to come. **Mark 10:21**

The young ruler's response was just like his fellow Pharisees.

"²² But he was sad at this word, and went away sorrowful, for he had great possessions." **Mark 10:22**

The young ruler's exuberance turned into sadness. His piety turned into sorrow at the Lord's response. This was a solemn disappointment since he didn't receive the eternal life he sought because the price of sacrifice was too high. He loved his earthly wealth more than the eternal life he sought, that is to say, more than he loved Jesus. He had no desire for the Lord of eternal life. He simply wanted to add eternal life to the laundry list of his self-accomplishments. This young man thought he had great possessions. What he did not realize was that he was a slave to those possessions.

³⁶ For what will it profit a man if he gains the whole world, and loses his own soul? ³⁷ Or what will a man give in exchange for

his soul? [38] For whoever is ashamed of Me and My words in this adulterous and sinful generation, of him the Son of Man also will be ashamed when He comes in the glory of His Father with the holy angels." **Mark 8:36-38**

Again, the lesson for us is not about the accumulation of earthly goods, as many in the Bible were rich, and others were living in abject poverty. The real question is: Do you love, and will you obey Jesus? David handled riches well, but his son Solomon used his wealth to purchase things the Lord said he should not because those things would turn his heart away from God.

"[23] Then Jesus looked around and said to His disciples, "How hard it is for those who have riches to enter the kingdom of God!" **Mark 10:23**

The word "hard" in this context means impossible. While "riches" have a propensity to propagate autonomy and a false sense of security, leading those who have riches to imagine they have no need for divine or heavenly resources. At that juncture, everything they do, and desire becomes earthly with no thought toward eternity or judgment.

"[22] Now he who received seed among the thorns is he who hears the word, and the cares of this world and the deceitfulness of riches choke the word, and he becomes unfruitful." **Matthew 13:22**

In the parable of the Sower, Jesus proclaims that all true believers are fruitful. "[23]But he who received seed on the good ground is he who hears the word and understands it, who indeed bears fruit and produces: some a hundredfold, some sixty, some thirty." **Matthew 13:23**

Unfortunately for the religious crowd like this young ruler, it also shows the utter uselessness and ineffectiveness of religion. No, I am not just speaking of Judaism but all the religions of the world. The rich young ruler's prominent position in the Synagogue, his knowledge and understanding of the proper scriptures (the Old Testament, which Jesus called scriptures), all his religious works, including giving of alms, could not bring peace to his heart or salvation for his soul. This is the main problem with works-based salvation. One will never know how much religious activity is enough to gain and keep this type of salvation, which is false salvation, by the way. How many prayers must be prayed? How many church services must be attended? How much money must be given? With how many people must we share the gospel? On and on and on it goes; when it stops, no one knows or ever will know. It is a vicious cycle invented by the devil and his wicked hoards to convince people that they can come to God by some form of human achievement as if that impresses a holy God. Satan has blinded their minds to the gospel and deceived them with false religion and self-righteousness.

"[12] Therefore, since we have such hope, we use great boldness of speech [13] unlike Moses, who put a veil over his face so that the children of Israel could not look steadily at the end of what was passing away. [14] But their minds were blinded. For until this day the same veil remains unlifted in the reading of the Old Testament, because the veil is taken away in Christ. [15] But even to this day, when Moses is read, a veil lies on their heart. [16] Nevertheless when one turns to the Lord, the veil is taken away. [17] Now the Lord is the Spirit; and where the Spirit of the Lord is, there is liberty. [18] But we all, with unveiled face, beholding as in a mirror the glory of the Lord, are being transformed into the same image from glory to glory, just as by the Spirit of the Lord." **2 Corinthians 3:12-18**

"³ But even if our gospel is veiled, it is veiled to those who are perishing, ⁴ whose minds the god of this age (Satan) has blinded, who do not believe, lest the light of the gospel of the glory of Christ, who is the image of God, should shine on them." **2 Corinthians 4:3-4**

Therein is the crux of the matter. Whose righteousness are you wearing? Jesus' righteousness comes by faith without any type or form of work. Human righteousness comes only by unclean works because of the flesh and is unacceptable to a holy God.

"³⁰What shall we say then? That Gentiles (non-Jews) who did not pursue righteousness, have attained to righteousness, even the righteousness of faith; ³¹ but Israel, pursuing the law of righteousness, has not attained to the law of righteousness. ³² Why? Because they did not seek it by faith, but as it were, by the works of the law. For they stumbled at that stumbling stone. ³³ As it is written: "Behold, I lay in Zion a stumbling stone and rock of offense, and whoever believes on Him will not be put to shame." Israel Needs the Gospel ¹ Brethren, my heart's desire and prayer to God for Israel is that they may be saved. ² For I bear them witness that **they have a zeal for God, but not according to knowledge**. ³ For they being ignorant of God's righteousness, and seeking to establish their own righteousness, have not submitted to the righteousness of God. ⁴ For Christ is the end of the law for righteousness to everyone who believes." **Romans 9:30-10:4**

Just like Nicodemus, who was afraid of being seen, came to Jesus by night with basically the same question and the same problem.

Jesus corrected his doctrine then preached the gospel, which Nicodemus eventually believed.

Does not the young ruler remind you of another young man, Saul of Tarsus? Both had an encounter with Jesus; however, the responses were totally opposite. Saul could have walked away from his experience, blind, of course, and returned to Jerusalem with his party, but he did not. Unlike the rich young ruler, Saul of Tarsus continued to seek out the person who confronted him about his sin.

You say: How do you know that?

From Paul's testimonies:

"³ For we are the circumcision, who worship God in the Spirit, rejoice in Christ Jesus, and have no confidence in the flesh, ⁴ though I also might have confidence in the flesh. If anyone else thinks he may have confidence in the flesh, I more so: ⁵ circumcised the eighth day, of the stock of Israel, of the tribe of Benjamin, a Hebrew of the Hebrews; concerning the law, a Pharisee; ⁶ concerning zeal, persecuting the church; concerning the righteousness which is in the law, blameless. ⁷ But what things were gain to me, these I have counted loss for Christ. ⁸ Yet indeed I also count all things loss for the excellence of the knowledge of Christ Jesus my Lord, for whom I have suffered the loss of all things, and count them as rubbish, that I may gain Christ ⁹ and be found in Him, not having my own righteousness, which is from the law, but that which is through faith in Christ, the righteousness which is from God by faith; ¹⁰ that I may know Him and the power of His resurrection, and the fellowship of His sufferings, being conformed to His death, ¹¹ if, by any means, I may attain to the resurrection from the dead." **Philippians 3:3-11**

What did he lack? Salvation! He was trusting his works, not the true meaning of the sacrifices, which represented Jesus' blood, shed on the cross.

"¹ For the law, having a shadow of the good things to come, and not the very image of the things, can never with these same sacrifices, which they offer continually year by year, make those who approach perfect." **Hebrews 10:1**

Paul wrote that those who had come to Christ by faith needed to continue in growth to maturity, enabling their minds to comprehend the wisdom of God imparted by the Holy Spirit.

"⁶ However, we speak wisdom among those who are mature, yet not the wisdom of this age, nor of the rulers of this age, who are coming to nothing." **1 Corinthians 2:6**

He described believers as "mature" when he referred to those whose righteousness was in Christ, as opposed to those who had confidence in the flesh.

¹ Finally, my brethren, rejoice in the Lord. For me to write the same things to you is not tedious, but for you it is safe. ² **Beware of dogs, beware of evil workers, beware of the mutilation**! ³ For we are the circumcision, who worship God in the Spirit, rejoice in Christ Jesus, and have no confidence in the flesh, ⁴ though I also might have confidence in the flesh. If anyone else thinks he may have confidence in the flesh, I more so: ⁵ circumcised the eighth day, of the stock of Israel, of the tribe of Benjamin, a Hebrew of the Hebrews; concerning the law, a Pharisee; ⁶ concerning zeal, persecuting the church; concerning the righteousness which is in the law, blameless. ⁷ But what things were gain to me, these I have counted loss for Christ. ⁸ Yet indeed I also count all things loss for the excellence of the knowledge

of Christ Jesus my Lord, for whom I have suffered the loss of all things, and count them as rubbish, that I may gain Christ [9] and be found in Him, not having my own righteousness, which is from the law, but that which is through faith in Christ, the righteousness which is from God by faith; [10] that I may know Him and the power of His resurrection, and the fellowship of His sufferings, being conformed to His death, [11] if, by any means, I may attain to the resurrection from the dead. [12] Not that I have already attained, or am already perfected; but I press on, that I may lay hold of that for which Christ Jesus has also laid hold of me. [13] Brethren, I do not count myself to have apprehended; but one thing I do, forgetting those things which are behind and reaching forward to those things which are ahead, [14] I press toward the goal for the prize of the upward call of God in Christ Jesus. [15] Therefore let us, as many as are mature, have this mind; and if in anything you think otherwise, God will reveal even this to you. [16] Nevertheless, to the degree that we have already attained, let us walk by the same rule, let us be of the same mind. Our Citizenship in Heaven [17] Brethren, join in following my example, and note those who so walk, as you have us for a pattern. [18] For many walk, of whom I have told you often, and now tell you even weeping, that they are the enemies of the cross of Christ: [19] whose end is destruction, whose god is their belly, and whose glory is in their shame who set their mind on earthly things. [20] For our citizenship is in heaven, from which we also eagerly wait for the Savior, the Lord Jesus Christ, [21] who will transform our lowly body that it may be conformed to His glorious body, according to the working by which He is able even to subdue all things to Himself. **Philippians 3:1-20**

Paul also declared that the apostles warned and taught everyone of the necessity of doctrinal study, which is required for spiritual growth in Christ.

"²⁴ I now rejoice in my sufferings for you, and fill up in my flesh what is lacking in the afflictions of Christ, for the sake of His body, which is the church, ²⁵ of which I became a minister according to the stewardship from God which was given to me for you, to fulfill the word of God, ²⁶ the mystery which has been hidden from ages and from generations, but now has been revealed to His saints. ²⁷ To them God willed to make known what are the riches of the glory of this mystery among the Gentiles: which is Christ in you, the hope of glory. ²⁸ Him we preach, warning every man and teaching every man in all wisdom, that we may present every man perfect in Christ Jesus." **Colossians 1:24-28**

"⁶ If you instruct the brethren in these things, you will be a good minister of Jesus Christ, nourished in the words of faith and of the good doctrine which you have carefully followed. ⁷ But reject profane and old wives' fables, and exercise yourself toward godliness. ⁸ For bodily exercise profits a little, but godliness is profitable for all things, having promise of the life that now is and of that which is to come. ⁹ This is a faithful saying and worthy of all acceptance. ¹⁰ For to this end, we both labor and suffer reproach, because we trust in the living God, who is the Savior of all men, especially of those who believe. ¹¹ These things command and teach." **1 Timothy 4:6-11**

Those who have come to Christ for spiritual completion are then trained by the Word and empowered by the Holy Spirit to discern truth from error and holy behavior from unholy.

"¹⁰ But you have carefully followed my doctrine, manner of life, purpose, faith, longsuffering, love, perseverance, ¹¹ persecutions, afflictions, which happened to me at Antioch, at Iconium, at Lystra what persecutions I endured. And out of them all the Lord delivered me. ¹² Yes, and all who desire to live godly in Christ Jesus will suffer persecution. ¹³ But evil men and impostors will grow worse and worse, deceiving and being deceived. ¹⁴ But you must continue in the things which you have learned and been assured of, knowing from whom you have learned them, ¹⁵ and that from childhood you have known the Holy Scriptures, which are able to make you wise for salvation through faith which is in Christ Jesus. ¹⁶ All Scripture is given by inspiration of God, and is profitable for doctrine, for reproof, for correction, for instruction in righteousness, ¹⁷ that the man of God may be complete, thoroughly equipped for every good work." **2 Timothy 3:10-17**

CHAPTER 2

THE TERROR OF HEBREWS 6

The problem most Christians have when reading the scriptures is that they confuse biblical references to fake believers and false prophets with references to true believers. The most popular biblical references are found in Hebrews 6, Hebrews 10, and 2 Peter 2. It would take a comprehensive study on these chapters to provide a complete contextual understanding; nevertheless, I will provide a brief synopsis. Let me begin by stating that everyone who holds the belief that these chapters teach that true born-again believers can lose their salvation due to works does not understand biblical salvation and is taking select verses completely out of their proper context.

You may say: You are sure being dogmatic, and that's a dogmatic statement.

Well, yes, I am, and it is intended to be. The Bible is a dogmatic book. There is only one God. There is only one way to this one God, through His Son, Jesus Christ. There is only one way to salvation, by grace through faith in Jesus Christ. Forgiveness of sins is provided only through the shedding of blood, Jesus' blood, period. No one receives forgiveness of their sins after believing in Christ because of good behavior. There is only one way to receive eternal life, by repentance and asking Jesus Christ to be your Savior and Lord. There is only one truth, the Bible, which declares that Jesus Christ is God who alone is creator, savior, and judge. All other ways, religions, religious books, and gods, are false and are an abomination to the One True God.

God does not ask you and I for our opinions. Paul charged all believers, "⁴ that you keep this commandment without spot, blameless until our Lord Jesus Christ's appearing, ¹⁵ which He will manifest in His own time, **who is the blessed and only Potentate**, the King of kings and Lord of lords, ¹⁶ who alone has immortality, dwelling in unapproachable light, whom no man has seen or can see, to whom be honor and everlasting power. Amen." **1 Timothy 6:14-16**

Can I tell you something that is a secret on earth to most people but is open scandal in heaven? Jesus is a Monarch, a Dictator, that is the meaning of Potentate. There are no committees or board of directors in heaven providing counsel to the Most High God. Does that offend you? Then you can always go and create your own universe, heaven, earth, and living creatures and rule over them, then set up as many committees and boards as you please. Until then, you and I will just have to obey the One who created us, the universe we live in, the heavens, the earth we live on, and all the living creatures that live therein. God never instructed me to apologize for Him being God therefore I will not. On the contrary, He instructed us to declare it.

"¹² Who has measured the waters in the hollow of His hand, measured heaven with a span and calculated the dust of the earth in a measure? Weighed the mountains in scales and the hills in a balance? ¹³ Who has directed the Spirit of the LORD, Or as His counselor has taught Him? [14] With whom did He take counsel, and who instructed Him, and taught Him in the path of justice? Who taught Him knowledge, and showed Him the way of understanding?" [17] All nations before Him are as nothing, and they are counted by Him less than nothing and worthless. [18] To whom then will you liken God? Or what likeness will you compare to Him? [28] Have you not known? Have you not heard? The everlasting God, the LORD, The Creator of the ends of the earth, neither faints nor is weary. His understanding is unsearchable." **Isaiah 40:12-14, 17-18, 28**

Listen to Nebuchadnezzar, King of Babylon, who once ruled the entire known world. He was a proud man strutting about in his magnificent royal palace, marveling at the glory of his own presence and power. He said to himself one day, in a moment of utter arrogance and pride, "is not this great Babylon, that I have built for a royal dwelling by my mighty power and for the honor of my majesty?"

What great swelling words and absolute contempt towards the Most High God! The Bible records, "[31]while the words were still in the king's mouth, a voice fell from heaven: "King Nebuchadnezzar, to you it is spoken: the kingdom has departed from you! [32]And they shall drive you from men, and your dwelling shall be with the be with the beasts of the field. They shall make you eat grass like oxen; and seven times shall pass over you, until you know that the Most High rules in the kingdom of men and gives it to whomever He chooses." Daniel 4:31-32

Do you think the king received the message after living outside like a cow for seven years? Listen to Ole King Nebuchadnezzar afterwards.

"³⁴ And at the end of the time I, Nebuchadnezzar, lifted my eyes to heaven, and my understanding returned to me; and I blessed the Most High and praised and honored Him who lives forever: For His dominion is an everlasting dominion, And His kingdom is from generation to generation. ³⁵ All the inhabitants of the earth are reputed as nothing; He does according to His will in the army of heaven and among the inhabitants of the earth. No one can restrain His hand or say to Him, "What have You done?" ³⁶ At the same time my reason returned to me, and for the glory of my kingdom, my honor and splendor returned to me. My counselors and nobles resorted to me, I was restored to my kingdom, and excellent majesty was added to me. ³⁷ Now I, Nebuchadnezzar, praise and extol and honor the King of heaven, all of whose works are truth, and His ways justice. And those who walk in pride He is able to put down." **Daniel 4:34-37**

Now addressing Hebrews 6. The context of Hebrews 6 actually begins in Hebrews 4 regarding Jesus being our great High Priest, with the key passage, with respect to our discussion, being Hebrews 5:14 and the usage of the phrase "of full age." "¹⁴ But solid food belongs to those who are of full age, that is, those who by reason of use have their senses exercised to discern both good and evil." **Hebrews 5:14**

The same Greek root for "of full age" is translated as "perfection" in **Hebrews 6:1** "¹ Therefore, leaving the discussion of the elementary principles of Christ, let us go on to perfection, not laying again the foundation of repentance from dead works and of faith toward God," and is elsewhere translated "perfect" in Hebrews 7:11, ¹¹ If perfection could have been attained through the Levitical priesthood and indeed the law given to the people established that priesthood why was there still need for another priest to come, one in the order of Melchizedek, not in the order of Aaron? It is evident that perfection used in these verses are not speaking of maturity. Rather, refers to salvation.

As a matter of fact, every time perfection is used in Hebrews, the reference is to salvation. Let us look at further examples in the book of Hebrews.

"¹⁹ for the law made nothing perfect; on the other hand, there is the bringing in of a better hope, through which we draw near to God." **Hebrews 7:19**

"²⁸ For the law appoints as high priests' men in all their weakness; but the oath, which came after the law, appointed the Son, who has been made perfect forever." **Hebrews 7:28**

"⁹ It was symbolic for the present time in which both gifts and sacrifices are offered which cannot make him who performed the service perfect in regard to the conscience." **Hebrews 9:9**

"¹ For the law, having a shadow of the good things to come, and not the very image of the things, can never with these same sacrifices, which they offer continually year by year, make those who approach perfect." **Hebrews 10:1**

"¹⁴ For by one offering He has perfected forever those who are being sanctified." **Hebrews 10:14**

"⁴⁰ God having provided something better for us, that they should not be made perfect apart from us." **Hebrews 11:40**

"²³ to the general assembly and church of the firstborn who are registered in heaven, to God the Judge of all, to the spirits of just men made perfect," **Hebrews 12:23**

It is used in Hebrews as a synonym for salvation, not maturity. In the context of Hebrews 5:14, it refers to the completion that comes when one becomes a believer in Christ, rather than referring to a Christian who has become mature, as is typical with Paul's writings as seen in Colossians 4:12.

"¹² Epaphras, who is one of you, a bondservant of Christ, greets you, always laboring fervently for you in prayers, that you may stand perfect and complete in all the will of God." **Colossians 4:12**

Do you see the difference?

First, Hebrews talks about Jesus' finished works at the cross, in the grave, and the resurrection, while Colossians refers to the believer's faith works.

Second, did you notice that every verse in Hebrews contains a definitive declaration by utilizing words such as "has perfected," "make perfect," or "made perfect?"

You say: What do you mean by definitive declaration?

I mean that the verses pronounce Jesus has done something on the believer's behalf that only He could do, the imputation of His righteousness, which has made us acceptable to the Father.

"⁵ But to him who does not work but believes on Him who **justifies the ungodly**, his faith is accounted for righteousness, ⁶ just as David also describes the **blessedness of the man to whom God imputes righteousness apart from works:** ⁷ "Blessed are those whose lawless deeds are forgiven, and whose sins are covered; ⁸ Blessed is the man to whom the LORD shall not impute sin." **Romans 4:5-8**

Please understand this, God does not justify godly people.

You ask: "why not?"

Because there are no godly people, only ungodly. You and I are gifted justification which ungodly people like us could never earn.

"³ Blessed be the God and Father of our Lord Jesus Christ, who has blessed us with every spiritual blessing in the heavenly places in Christ, ⁴ just as He chose us in Him before the foundation of the world, that we should be holy and without blame before Him in love, ⁵ having predestined us to adoption as sons by Jesus Christ to Himself, according to the good pleasure of His will, ⁶ to the praise of the glory of His grace, **by which He made us accepted in the Beloved.**" **Ephesians 1:3-6**

The writer of Hebrews encourages the Jewish unbelievers to leave the elementary principles of Christ.

You may be thinking: What are the elementary principles of Christ?

The things contained in the Old Testament laws, statutes, and ordinances, some of which are listed in verses 1 and 2. One can find the entire list by reading the books of Exodus, Leviticus, Numbers, and Deuteronomy, as well as the New Testament book of Colossians.

"¹ Therefore, leaving the discussion of the elementary principles of Christ, let us go on to perfection, not laying again the foundation of **repentance from dead works** and of **faith toward God,** ² of the **doctrine of baptisms**, of **laying on of hands**, of **resurrection of the dead**, and of **eternal judgment.**" **Hebrews 6:1-2**

No, laying on of hands in this verse has nothing to do with healing or transferring of power or any such thing. All these items are Old Testament types and shadows of Christ's offering himself for sin. Let us examine the ordinances of the Law from the Old Testament scriptures, which the Jewish audience would have understood.

"¹ Moreover, brethren, I do not want you to be unaware that all our fathers were under the cloud, all passed through the sea, ² **all were baptized into Moses** in the cloud and in the sea, ³ all ate the same spiritual food, ⁴ and all drank the same spiritual drink. For they drank of that spiritual Rock that followed them, and that Rock was Christ." **1 Corinthians 10:1-4**

"¹⁵ And the elders of the congregation shall lay their hands on the head of the bull before the LORD. Then the bull shall be killed before the LORD." **Leviticus 4:15**

"²¹ Aaron shall lay both his hands on the head of the live goat, confess over it all the iniquities of the children of Israel, and all their transgressions, concerning all their sins, putting them on the head of the goat, and shall send it away into the wilderness by the hand of a suitable man." **Leviticus 16:21**

"¹² Then the Levites shall lay their hands on the heads of the young bulls, and you shall offer one as a sin offering and the other as a burnt offering to the LORD, to make atonement for the Levites." **Numbers 8:12**

In Galatians, Paul outlined the purpose for the law, providing more evidence that the law could not and never made anyone perfect before God, no matter how diligent they were at keeping the law. Paul even declared to the church at Corinth that he was blameless when it came to following the law, but he was lost as a breath of air in a hurricane.

"¹⁹ What purpose then does the law serve? It was added because of transgressions, till the Seed should come to whom the promise was made; and it was appointed through angels by the hand of a mediator. ²⁰ Now a mediator does not mediate for one only, but God is one.

²¹ Is the law then against the promises of God? Certainly not! For if there had been a law given which could have given life, truly righteousness would have been by the law. ²² But the Scripture has confined all under sin, that the promise by faith in Jesus Christ might be given to those who believe. ²³ But before faith came, we were kept under guard by the law, kept for the faith which would afterward be revealed. ²⁴ **Therefore the law was our tutor to bring us to Christ, that we might be justified by faith. ²⁵ But after faith has come, we are no longer under a tutor." Galatians 3:19-25**

These Jewish men and women were being instructed to leave the old system of law and animal sacrifices, which could never take away sins and embrace the true Lamb of God who can and did. They were not saved because they had not transitioned from Moses to Christ, from covered sins to eradicated sins.

Now that we have the context, let us examine the main verses of Hebrews 6 that are used to scare Christians to death.

"⁴ For it is impossible for those who were once enlightened, and have tasted of the heavenly gift, and were made partakers of the Holy Ghost, ⁵ And have tasted the good word of God, and the powers of the world to come, ⁶ If they shall fall away, to renew them again unto repentance; seeing they crucify to themselves the Son of God afresh, and put him to an open shame." **Hebrews 6:4-6**

Notice that the writer is addressing his commentary to "those."

Who are "those"?

The Jewish people who were still offering animal sacrifices and following the law. Remember, the temple was still operational when the book of Hebrews was written around A.D. 67-69.

How then were they once enlightened? When did they taste the heavenly gift? When did they partake of the Holy Ghost? When did they taste the good word of God and the powers of the world to come?

I will let Moses and Paul explain this to you. Again, for contextual purposes and for those without Bibles, extended excerpts are included.

Moses:

"[32] Ask now about the former days, long before your time, from the day God created human beings on the earth; ask from one end of the heavens to the other. Has anything so great as this ever happened, or has anything like it ever been heard of? [33] **Has any other people heard the voice of God speaking out of fire, as you have, and lived?** [34] Has any god ever tried to take for himself one nation out of another nation, **by testings, by signs and wonders, by war, by a mighty hand and an outstretched arm, or by great and awesome deeds, like all the things the LORD your God did for you in Egypt before your very eyes?**

³⁵ **You were shown these things so that you might know that the LORD is God; besides him there is no other.** ³⁶ **From heaven he made you hear his voice to discipline you. On earth he showed you his great fire, and you heard his words from out of the fire.** ³⁷ Because he loved your ancestors and chose their descendants after them, he brought you out of Egypt by his Presence and his great strength, ³⁸ to drive out before you nations greater and stronger than you and to bring you into their land to give it to you for your inheritance, as it is today.

³⁹ Acknowledge and take to heart this day that the LORD is God in heaven above and on the earth below. There is no other. ⁴⁰ Keep his decrees and commands, which I am giving you today, so that it may go well with you and your children after you and that you may live long in the land the LORD your God gives you for all time." **Deuteronomy 4:32-40**

"²² These are the commandments the LORD proclaimed in a loud voice to your whole assembly there on the mountain from out of the fire, the cloud and the deep darkness; and he added nothing more. Then he wrote them on two stone tablets and gave them to me.

²³ When you heard the voice out of the darkness, while the mountain was ablaze with fire, all the leaders of your tribes and your elders came to me. ²⁴ And you said, **"The LORD our God has shown us his glory and his majesty, and we have heard his voice from the fire.** Today we have seen that a person can live even if God speaks with them. ²⁵ But now, why should we die? This great fire will consume us, and we will die if we hear the voice of the LORD our God any longer. ²⁶ For what mortal has ever heard the voice of the living God speaking out of fire, as we

have, and survived? [27] Go near and listen to all that the LORD our God says. Then tell us whatever the LORD our God tells you. We will listen and obey." **Deuteronomy 5:22-27**

"[20] "See, **I am sending an angel ahead of you to guard you along the way** and to bring you to the place I have prepared. [21] Pay attention to him and listen to what he says. Do not rebel against him; he will not forgive your rebellion, since **my Name is in him**. [22] If you listen carefully to what he says and do all that I say, I will be an enemy to your enemies and will oppose those who oppose you. [23] My angel will go ahead of you and bring you into the land of the Amorites, Hittites, Perizzites, Canaanites, Hivites and Jebusites, and I will wipe them out." **Exodus 23:20-23**

[1] Then the LORD said to Moses, [2] **"See, I have chosen Bezalel son of Uri, the son of Hur, of the tribe of Judah,** [3] **and I have filled him with the Spirit of God, with wisdom, with understanding, with knowledge and with all kinds of skills** [4] to make artistic designs for work in gold, silver and bronze, [5] to cut and set stones, to work in wood, and to engage in all kinds of crafts. [6] Moreover, I have appointed Oholiab son of Ahisamak, of the tribe of Dan, to help him. Also I have given ability to all the skilled workers to make everything I have commanded you: [7] the tent of meeting, the ark of the covenant law with the atonement cover on it, and all the other furnishings of the tent [8] the table and its articles, the pure gold lampstand and all its accessories, the altar of incense, [9] the altar of burnt offering and all its utensils, the basin with its stand [10] and also the woven garments, both the sacred garments for Aaron the priest and the garments for his sons when they serve as priests, [11] and the anointing oil and fragrant incense for the Holy Place. They are to make them just as I commanded you." **Exodus 31:1-11**

Paul:

"³⁷ "This is the Moses who told the Israelites, 'God will raise up for you a prophet like me from your own people.' ³⁸ He was in the assembly in the wilderness, **with the angel (Jesus, the Angel of the Lord) who spoke to him on Mount Sinai,** and with our ancestors; and he received living words to pass on to us." **Acts 7:37-38**

"¹ What advantage, then, is there in being a Jew, or what value is there in circumcision? ² Much in every way! First of all, **the Jews have been entrusted with the very words of God**." **Romans 3:1-2**

"¹ I speak the truth in Christ I am not lying, my conscience confirms it through the Holy Spirit ² I have great sorrow and unceasing anguish in my heart. ³ For I could wish that I myself were cursed and cut off from Christ for the sake of my people, those of my own race, ⁴ the people of Israel. Theirs is the **adoption to sonship; theirs the divine glory, the covenants, the receiving of the law, the temple worship, and the promises**. ⁵ Theirs are the patriarchs, and from them is traced **the human ancestry of the Messiah, who is God** over all, forever praised! Amen." **Romans 9:1-5**

Saul, David, and Solomon, kings of Israel, all had the Holy Spirit upon them, not in them. In Psalm 51, after sinning against the Lord with Bathsheba, David cried out to the Lord not to take the Holy Spirit from him.

"⁹ Hide your face from my sins and blot out all my iniquity. ¹⁰ Create in me a pure heart, O God, and renew a steadfast spirit within me. ¹¹ Do not cast me from your presence or take **your Holy**

Spirit from me. ¹² **Restore to me the joy of your salvation** and grant me a willing spirit, to sustain me." **Psalms 51:9-12**

David was asking God to spare his life as the penalty for breaking all ten commandments was death. Notice that David asked the Lord to restore unto him the joy of salvation, not salvation. David understood that it was impossible for him to lose his salvation. David was especially anointed, as he was both prophet and king. Only Christ though was, and is, and shall forever be Apostle, High Priest, Prophet, and King.

The Holy Spirit was with Abraham and Isaac, and upon Jacob. As testified by Peter, all the holy prophets had the Holy Spirit upon them, including Moses.

"²⁰ Above all, you must understand that no prophecy of Scripture came about by the prophet's own interpretation of things. ²¹ For prophecy never had its origin in the human will, but prophets, though human, spoke from God as they were carried along by the Holy Spirit." **2 Peter 1:20-21**

Back to our text.

"⁶ If they shall fall away, to renew them again unto repentance; seeing they crucify to themselves the Son of God afresh and put him to an open shame." **Hebrews 6:6**

Who are "they"?

They are the Jews, the Hebrews.

Fall away from what?

Fall away from the truth of the gospel. This was referenced in chapter 2.

"¹ We must pay the most careful attention, therefore, to what we have heard, so that we do not drift away. ² For since the message spoken through angels was binding,

When was the message spoken through angels?

During the wilderness journey to the promise land.

and every violation and disobedience received its just punishment, ³ how shall we escape if we ignore so great a salvation? This salvation, which was first announced by the Lord, was confirmed to us by those who heard him. ⁴ God also testified to it by signs, wonders and various miracles, and by gifts of the Holy Spirit distributed according to his will." **Hebrews 2:1-4**

The Jews were willfully ignoring the salvation preached by Jesus and then by the apostles and prophets of the early church. The writer of the book of Hebrews continued to warn the Jews about being unbelievers in chapter 3.

"¹² See to it, brothers and sisters (the writer was also Jewish), that none of you has a sinful, unbelieving heart that turns away from the living God. ¹³ But encourage one another daily, as long as it is called "Today," so that none of you may be hardened by sin's deceitfulness. ¹⁴ We have come to share in Christ, if indeed we hold our original conviction firmly to the very end. ¹⁵ As has just been said: "Today, if you hear his voice, do not harden your hearts as you did in the rebellion." ¹⁶ Who were they who heard and rebelled? Were they not all those Moses led out of Egypt? ¹⁷ And with whom was he angry for forty years? Was it not with those who sinned, whose bodies perished in the wilderness? ¹⁸ And to whom did God swear that they would never enter his rest if not to those who disobeyed? [19] So we see that they were not able to enter, because of their unbelief." **Hebrews 3:12-19**

The warning is about not believing the gospel of Christ, that Jesus was the Jewish Messiah. It was extremely difficult for the Jews because they were taught that the Messiah will come and rid the world of their enemies and commence the kingdom age immediately. Even the disciples believed this until after the resurrection. Note that only the unbelievers perished in the wilderness.

It is the same message Paul gave to the church at Corinth. Examine yourself to see if you are in the faith. He had reasons to doubt that they were saved because of their behavior and lack of spiritual growth.

"[5] Examine yourselves to see whether you are in the faith; test yourselves. Do you not realize that Christ Jesus is in you unless, of course, you fail the test? [6] And I trust that you will discover that we have not failed the test." **2 Corinthians 13:5-6**

Why did Paul have to challenge their belief in Christ?

You must revert to chapter 12 for that answer.

[19] Have you been thinking all along that we have been defending ourselves to you? We have been speaking in the sight of God as those in Christ; and everything we do, dear friends, is for your strengthening. [20] **For I am afraid that when I come, I may not find you as I want you to be, and you may not find me as you want me to be. I fear that there may be discord, jealousy, fits of rage, selfish ambition, slander, gossip, arrogance, and disorder.** [21] I am afraid that when I come again my God will humble me before you, and **I will be grieved over many who have**

sinned earlier and have not repented of the impurity, sexual sin, and debauchery in which they have indulged.

[1] This will be my third visit to you. "Every matter must be established by the testimony of two or three witnesses." [2] I already gave you a warning when I was with you the second time. I now repeat it while absent: On my return **I will not spare those who sinned earlier or any of the others,** [3] **since you are demanding proof that Christ is speaking through me.** He is not weak in dealing with you but is powerful among you. [4] For to be sure, he was crucified in weakness, yet he lives by God's power. Likewise, we are weak in him, yet **by God's power we will live with him in our dealing with you**. 2 Corinthians 12:19-13:4

Overt sins were being committed by members of the church, who were not repenting, and no one was condemning it. Beloved that cannot be in the church of the Most High God. The apostle recognized the fruitlessness and had to challenge their faith in Christ because true saving faith always lead to a changed lifestyle.

Back to Hebrews 6. Who had an unbelieving heart?

Most of the Jews had unbelieving hearts. They wanted to believe; however, they were too afraid of being ostracized by family and friends and excommunicated by the religious leaders then thrown out of the temple. This was no easy decision for the Jews in those days as they did not leave the family house like we do today, and they were taught all their lives that animal sacrifice was the only way to get forgiveness of sins. Believing in Jesus means you would lose everything, even your life. Most of these people were present when Jesus was performing the miracles in Israel. They had firsthand knowledge of the Lord but did not see him after the resurrection because Christ only showed himself and was touched by those who loved Him. Never again will any unbelieving wicked person touch the Holy One.

Due to their lack of understanding of the scriptures, like most in Israel, they had trouble believing in a Messiah that could die. They were constantly told about a Messiah that will restore the kingdom to Israel. That is why Judas betrayed Christ. That is what confused the disciples when the Lord began talking about the cross. They knew He was God and could not understand how God could die. Most Jews believed Jesus would lead the rebellion against the Romans, but once He was arrested, they thought He was another fake Messiah. Note how they mocked Him on the cross.

"[39] And those who passed by blasphemed Him, wagging their heads [40] and saying, "You who destroy the temple and build it in three days, save Yourself! If You are the Son of God, come down from the cross." [41] Likewise the chief priests also, mocking with the scribes and elders, said, [42] "He saved others; Himself He cannot save. If He is the King of Israel, let Him now come down from the cross, and we will believe Him. [43] He trusted in God; let Him deliver Him now if He will have Him; for He said, 'I am the Son of God.'" **Matthew 27:39-43**

Jesus said, "[24] I told you that you would die in your sins; if you do not believe that I, am he, you will indeed die in your sins." **John 8:24**

Unfortunately, many stopped following Jesus, returned to the law, and offered sacrifices that represented Christ. This they did after the resurrection, thereby making a conscious decision and confirming their unbelief in the risen Savior.

They fell away from the truth of the gospel and crucified the Son of God again by offering animal sacrifices, which is a type and shadow of Christ, thereby publicly denouncing him. This wicked act only confirmed that they did not believe in Jesus.

"⁴For it is impossible for those who were once enlightened, and have tasted the heavenly gift, and have become partakers of the Holy Spirit, ⁵ and have tasted the good word of God and the powers of the age to come, ⁶ if they fall away, to renew them again to repentance, since they crucify again for themselves the Son of God and put Him to an open shame." **Hebrews 6:4-6**

Believers are charged to publicly declare our allegiance to Christ. Some of these Jews were doing just the opposite.

Jesus said, ""³² "Whoever acknowledges me before others, I will also acknowledge before my Father in heaven. ³³ But whoever disowns me before others, I will disown before my Father in heaven. ³⁴ "Do not suppose that I have come to bring peace to the earth. I did not come to bring peace, but a sword. ³⁵ For I have come to turn "'a man against his father, a daughter against her mother, a daughter-in-law against her mother-in-law ³⁶ a man's enemies will be the members of his own household.' ³⁷ "Anyone who loves their father or mother more than me is not worthy of me; anyone who loves their son or daughter more than me is not worthy of me. ³⁸ Whoever does not take up their cross and follow me is not worthy of me. ³⁹ Whoever finds their life will lose it, and whoever loses their life for my sake will find it." **Matthew 10:32-39**

The "for it is impossible" in Hebrews 6:4 has a clear connection with the "to renew them again to repentance" of Hebrews 6:6.

Those who sinned against Christ with their eyes wide open had no hope of restoration or forgiveness.

You may ask: Why not?

Well, the reason is found in Hebrews 6:5-6, they had rejected Jesus with full knowledge of who He was and conscious experience. Just like the Pharisees, these Jews, with full revelation from seeing Jesus, the witness of apostles, and the revelation from the Holy Spirit, they rejected the truth concerning Jesus, therefore, had no hope of being saved. They could never have more knowledge than they had when they rejected it. They have concluded that Jesus' claim to be the Jewish Messiah was false, hence blasphemous; therefore, He should have been crucified, and they stand aligned with His enemies. These Jews, and all others like them, reject the only prescribed way God has provided for people to be saved.

Why the urgency?

Because only a few years later, the temple and Jerusalem were burned to the ground by the Romans, with the scrolls (most) and genealogies being lost forever and the animal sacrifices ceased. Over one million Jews died, and all others expelled from the promised land.

Hebrews 6:7-8 confirms what I just explained. Rain falls to the earth where all seeds are watered; however, some seeds cultivate and produce fruit while others cultivate yet produce thorns and briers. The fruitful believer receives the blessings that God the Father bestows upon His Son, Jesus, while the thorny unbeliever receives the curses and wrath of God intended for their father, the devil, which is being cast into the lake of fire.

⁷ For the earth which drinks in the rain that often comes upon it, and bears herbs useful for those by whom it is cultivated, receives blessing from God; ⁸ but if it bears thorns and briers, it is rejected and near to being cursed, whose end is to be burned. **Hebrews 6:7-8**

There is no possibility that these verses remotely refer to losing salvation. There are far too many scriptural passages that make it unmistakably clear that salvation is eternal (John 10:27-29; Rom. 8:35, 38, 39; Phil. 1:6; 1 Pet. 1:4, 5), to name a few.

If you who desire to make this verse mean that true believers can lose their eternal salvation, then you will need to conclude that once salvation is lost by committing any sin, it would then, by that interpretation, be impossible to reacquire according to Hebrews 6:6. You cannot say that according to verse 4, salvation can be lost, then turn around and state that it can be recovered through confession and repentance, totally ignoring verse 6. According to this passage, if salvation is ever lost, it can never be regained. Beloved, the Bible does not teach that doctrine.

Hopefully, you now understand that the writer was speaking to unbelieving Jews who would have understood the message. This is clearly confirmed in Hebrews 6:9-10 as the writer begins to address believers by calling them beloved, then states that they are confident of better things concerning you (believers), in things that accompany salvation, which are the works of faith through love that are evidence of saving faith. The writer then lists the evidence.

"⁹ But, **beloved**, we are confident of better things concerning you, yes, **things that accompany salvation**, though we speak in this manner. ¹⁰ For God is not unjust to forget **your work** and **labor**

of love which you have shown toward His name, in that you have **ministered to the saints**, and **do minister**." **Hebrews 6:9-10**

1. Work of faith in the Holy Spirit
2. Labor of love toward Jesus
3. Love of fellow believers
4. Service to fellow believers

Finally, in verses 11 and 12, true saving faith brings a full assurance of salvation and the preservation of the saints.

"[11] And we desire that each one of you show the same diligence to the **full assurance of hope until the end**, [12] that you do not become sluggish, but imitate those who through faith and patience **inherit the promises**." **Hebrews 6:11-12**

Ultimately if believers continue patiently in faithful works of love, we all will receive the promised inheritance described beautifully in 1 Cor. 3 and 2 Cor. 5.

"[5] What, after all, is Apollos? And what is Paul? Only servants, through whom you came to believe as the Lord has assigned to each his task. [6] I planted the seed, Apollos watered it, but God has been making it grow. [7] So neither the one who plants nor the one who waters is anything, but only God, who makes things grow. [8] The one who plants and the one who waters have one purpose, and they will each be rewarded according to their own labor. [9] For we are co-workers in God's service; you are God's field, God's building. [10] By the grace God has given me, I laid a foundation as a wise builder, and someone else is building on it. But each one should build with care. [11] For no one can lay any foundation other than the one already laid, which is Jesus Christ. [12] If anyone builds on this foundation using **gold, silver, costly stones**, wood, hay, or straw, [13] their work will be shown for what it is, because the Day will bring it to light. It will be revealed with fire, and the fire will test the quality of each person's work. [14] **If what has been built survives, the builder will receive a reward.** [15] If it is burned up, the builder will suffer loss but yet will be saved even though only as one escaping through the flames. **1 Corinthians 3:5-15**

"[9]So we make it our goal to please him, whether we are at home in the body or away from it. [10] For we must all appear before the judgment seat of Christ, so that each of us may receive what is due us for the things done while in the body, whether good or bad. **2 Corinthians 5:9-11**

That was much more detail than I originally planned to provide. Now, let us transition briefly to Hebrews 10.

CHAPTER 3

THE TREPIDATION OF HEBREWS 10

Hebrews 10 has caused countless believers to suffer from sleep deprivation. Throughout the years, there have been numerous sermons preached around this chapter that have left even some mature Christians doubting their assurance of salvation. Most messages preached about Hebrews 10 most assuredly lean on the connotation that believers who willfully sin will lose their salvation and must do some form of penance to return to the good graces of our Lord. They would also say that it is not possible to be certain that you possess eternal life, which some call eternal security or, once saved always saved.

The problem with this view toward eternal life is, by mere definition, if something that is eternal can be taken away or forfeited, then it cannot be eternal. Again, it is not my intent to discuss eternal salvation and its meaning. However, considering our text, the topic must be breached if only to correct the incorrect interpretation of Hebrews 10.

The warning in this passage deals expressly with the sin of apostasy, an intentional falling away, or defection. Apostates are those who move toward Christ, hear, and understand His gospel, and are on the verge of saving belief, but then rebel and turn away.

This warning against apostasy is one of the most serious warnings in all of scripture. Not all the Jews would respond to the gentle invitation of vv. 19-25. Some were already beyond response. Hebrews 10:26

Now reading our text.

"²⁶For if we sin willfully after we have received the knowledge of the truth, there no longer remains a sacrifice for sins, ²⁷ but a certain fearful expectation of judgment, and fiery indignation which will devour the adversaries. ²⁸ Anyone who has rejected Moses' law dies without mercy on the testimony of two or three witnesses. ²⁹ Of how much worse punishment, do you suppose, will he be thought worthy who has trampled the Son of God underfoot, counted the blood of the covenant by which he was sanctified a common thing, and insulted the Spirit of grace? ³⁰ For we know Him who said, "Vengeance is Mine, I will repay," says the Lord. And again, "The LORD will judge His people." ³¹ It is a fearful thing to fall into the hands of the living God." **Hebrews 10:26-29**

The writer is speaking rhetorically.

You say: How did you come to that conclusion?

Well, like Hebrews 6, where the writer changes audience, the writer does it again in verse 39 of chapter 10. He excludes himself and genuine believers from this group that willfully sin. The Greek term denotes the notion of deliberate intentional and habitual sin. The question is, what sin is being referenced?

The sin of deliberately rejecting Christ.

You may ask: How do you know that?

From the context and the reading of Pentateuch (i.e., Genesis, Exodus, Leviticus, Numbers, and Deuteronomy). That is why it is extremely important that we read the entire Bible. In the Old Testament, we find why God instituted animal sacrifices first to Adam and his believing descendants, then for the nation of Israel through whom our Savior came. In the New Testament, God reveals the mystery and completes His master plan for salvation.

"[1] The law is only a shadow of the good things that are coming—not the realities themselves. For this reason, it can never, by the same sacrifices repeated endlessly year after year, make perfect those who draw near to worship. [2] Otherwise, would they not have stopped being offered? For the worshipers would have been cleansed once for all and would no longer have felt guilty for their sins. [3] But those sacrifices are an annual reminder of sins. [4] It is impossible for the blood of bulls and goats to take away sins. [5] Therefore, when Christ came into the world, he said: "Sacrifice and offering you did not desire, but a body you prepared for me; [6] with burnt offerings and sin offerings you were not pleased. [7] Then I said, 'Here I am it is written about me in the scroll I have come to do your will, my God.'" [8] First he said, "Sacrifices and offerings, burnt offerings and sin offerings you did not desire, nor were you pleased with them" though they were offered in accordance with the law. [9] Then he said, "Here I am, I have come to do your will." He sets aside the first to establish the second. [10] And by that will, we have been made holy through the sacrifice of the body of Jesus Christ once for all. [11] Day after day every priest stands and performs his religious duties; again, and again he offers the same sacrifices, which can never take away sins. [12] But when this priest had offered for all time one sacrifice for sins, he sat down at the right hand of God, [13] and since that time he waits for his enemies to be made his footstool. [14] For by one sacrifice he has made perfect forever those who are being made holy. [15] The Holy Spirit also testifies to us about this. First, he says: [16] "This is the covenant I will make with them after that time, says the Lord. I will put my laws in their hearts, and I will write them on their minds." [17] Then he adds: "Their sins and lawless acts I will remember no more." [18] And where these have been forgiven, sacrifice for sin is no longer necessary." **Hebrews 10:1-18**

This was beautifully displayed in the book of Leviticus. We read in Leviticus 1.

[3] "'If the offering is a burnt offering from the herd (the process was a little different for sheep, goats, or birds but the meaning was the same), you are to offer a male without defect. (Defect represents sin and Christ had no sin) You must present it at the entrance (Christ is the door) to the tent of meeting (no entrance was granted until the sacrifice was offered) so that it will be acceptable to the LORD. [4] You are to lay your hand on the head of the burnt offering (representing the transfer of sins from the guilty to the innocent. From us to Christ), and it will be accepted on your behalf to make atonement (covering of sins not removal) for you. You are to slaughter the young bull (we slaughter Christ with our sins) before the LORD, and then Aaron's sons the priests shall bring the blood and splash it against the sides of the altar at the entrance to the tent of meeting. (Christ our High Priest presents his own blood to the Father) [6] You are to skin the burnt offering and cut it into pieces. [7] The sons of Aaron the priest are to put fire on the altar and arrange wood on the fire. [8] Then Aaron's sons the priests shall arrange the pieces, including the head and the fat, on the wood that is burning on the altar. [9] You are to wash the internal organs and the legs with water (blood and water from the sacrifice), and the priest is to burn

all of it on the altar. It is a burnt offering, a food offering, an aroma pleasing to the LORD." **Leviticus 1:3-9**

Is not that a beautiful picture of our Lord on the cross? Compare that with Hebrews 10:19-25.

"[19] Therefore, brethren, having boldness to enter the Holiest by the blood of Jesus, [20] by a new and living way which He consecrated for us, through the veil, that is, His flesh, [21] and having a High Priest over the house of God, [22] **let us draw near with a true heart in full assurance of faith, having our hearts sprinkled from an evil conscience and our bodies washed with pure water**. [23] Let us hold fast the confession of our hope without wavering, for He who promised is faithful. [24] And let us consider one another in order to stir up love and good works, [25] not forsaking the assembling of ourselves together, as is the manner of some, but exhorting one another, and so much the more as you see the Day approaching." **Hebrews 10:19-25**

"[33] But when they came to Jesus and found that he was already dead, they did not break his legs. [34] Instead, one of the soldiers pierced Jesus' side with a spear, bringing a sudden flow of blood and water." **John 19:33-34**

Blood to redeem and water to cleanse! Oh, Father, hallowed be Your name.

We continue in Leviticus 2 with the grain offering, which was only presented to the Lord after the burnt offering.

Why?

The grain offering represented worship and God cannot accept worship from unclean (sin-filled) hearts and hands.

"¹ 'When anyone offers a grain offering to the LORD, his offering shall be of fine flour. And he shall pour oil on it and put frankincense on it. ² He shall bring it to Aaron's sons, the priests, one of whom shall take from it his handful of fine flour and oil with all the frankincense. And the priest shall burn it as a memorial on the altar, an offering made by fire, a sweet aroma to the LORD. ³ The rest of the grain offering shall be Aaron's and his sons'. It is most holy of the offerings to the LORD made by fire. ⁴ "'If you bring a grain offering baked in an oven, it is to consist of the finest flour: either thick loaves made without yeast and with olive oil mixed in or thin loaves made without yeast and brushed with olive oil. ⁵ If your grain offering is prepared on a griddle, it is to be made of the finest flour mixed with oil, and without yeast. ⁶ Crumble it and pour oil on it; it is a grain offering. ⁷ If your grain offering is cooked in a pan, it is to be made of the finest flour and some olive oil. ⁸ Bring the grain offering made of these things to the LORD; present it to the priest, who shall take it to the altar. ⁹ He shall take out the memorial portion from the grain offering and burn it on the altar as a food offering, an aroma pleasing to the LORD. ¹⁰ The rest of the grain offering belongs to Aaron and his sons; it is a most holy part of the food offerings presented to the LORD." **Leviticus 2:1-10**

Now that we are finally cleansed from our sins, we are free to offer worship to our Lord, who is holy.

Beloved, it is extremely difficult to get a more beautiful picture of worship in the word of God than this. Please allow me to expound.

1. With oil—is the way we walk, teach, and pray in the Holy Spirit.

"¹⁶ I say then: Walk in the Spirit, and you shall not fulfill the lust of the flesh." **Galatians 5:16**

"²⁰ But you, beloved, building yourselves up on your most holy faith, praying in the Holy Spirit," **Jude 1:20**

²⁷ As for you, the anointing you received from him remains in you, and you do not need anyone to teach you. But as his anointing teaches you about all things and as that anointing is real, not counterfeit—just as it has taught you, remain in him." **1 John 2:27**

    2. Oil upon—we are baptized into the body of Christ by the Holy Spirit.

"¹³ For by one Spirit we were all baptized into one body whether Jews or Greeks, whether slaves or free and have all been made to drink into one Spirit." **1 Corinthians 12:13**

    3. Mixed with oil—we are born again of the Spirit and are the temple of the Holy Spirit.

"⁵Jesus answered, "Very truly I tell you, no one can enter the kingdom of God unless they are born of water and the Spirit. ⁶ Flesh gives birth to flesh, but the Spirit gives birth to spirit." **John 3:5-6**

"¹⁹ Or do you not know that your body is the temple of the Holy Spirit who is in you, whom you have from God, and you are not your own? ²⁰ For you were bought at a price; therefore, glorify God in your body and in your spirit, which are God's." **1 Corinthians 6:19-20**

    4. Pour oil there on—we are led by the Holy Spirit

"¹⁴ For those who are led by the Spirit of God are the children of God." **Romans 8:14**

Frankincense only releases its fragrance when it is crushed, beaten, pressured, or burned. This represents us suffering with Christ, baring our cross in humble service to our Lord.

"¹⁴ Now thanks be to God who always leads us in triumph in Christ, and through us diffuses the fragrance of His knowledge in every place. ¹⁵ For we are to God the fragrance of Christ among those who are being saved and among those who are perishing." **2 Corinthians 2:14-15**

The priests received a portion of the meal offering. We are instructed to eat the body of Christ and drink his blood, which represents the word of God as our food and drink like the deer that pants after the water brooks. The blood of Jesus perpetually cleanses us from sin while our Lord, using the water of the word of God, washes our feet while we, as pilgrims and strangers, journey through this world. Dressed in the armor of God, daily combatting the impurities of our flesh, uncleanness of this sin filled world, and the fiery darts of temptation from the devil and his legions of demons.

"⁷But if we walk in the light as He is in the light, we have fellowship with one another, and the blood of Jesus Christ His Son cleanses us from all sin." **1 John 1:7**

"²⁵ Husbands, love your wives, just as Christ also loved the church and gave Himself for her, ²⁶ that He might sanctify and cleanse her with the washing of water by the word, ²⁷ that He might present her to Himself a glorious church, not having spot or wrinkle or any such thing, but that she should be holy and without blemish." **Ephesians 5:25-27**

The priests were instructed to eat the remainder of the grain offering. Therefore, we should long and thirst after the word until we are consumed with our hearts filled to keep us from sins, and minds renewed to think God's thoughts after Him.

"¹⁵ Be diligent (study) to present yourself approved to God, a worker who does not need to be ashamed, rightly dividing the word of truth." **2 Timothy 2:15**

There was to be no leaven, as it represents sin. We are to live holy lives, well-pleasing to our heavenly Father and our Lord Jesus Christ as we follow Him in humble obedience in the power of the Holy Spirit.

"¹³ Therefore, with minds that are alert and fully sober, set your hope on the grace to be brought to you when Jesus Christ is revealed at his coming. ¹⁴ As obedient children do not conform to the evil desires you had when you lived in ignorance. ¹⁵ But just as he who called you is holy, so be holy in all you do; ¹⁶ for it is written: "Be holy, because I am holy."" **1 Peter 1:13-16**

Salt was to be added, which speaks of us, as slaves of Christ, being faithful in our service to the One who is faithful and true.

"¹Let a man so consider us, as slaves of Christ and stewards of the mysteries of God. ² Moreover it is required in stewards that one be found faithful." **1 Corinthians 4:1-2**

"⁹ God is faithful, by whom you were called into the fellowship of His Son, Jesus Christ our Lord." **1 Corinthians 1:9**

"⁴ Grace and peace to you from him who is, and who was, and who is to come, and from the seven spirits before his throne, ⁵ and from Jesus Christ, who is the faithful witness, the firstborn from the dead, and the ruler of the kings of the earth. To him who loves us and has freed us from our sins by his blood, ⁶ and has made us to be a kingdom and priests to serve his God and Father to him be glory and power for ever and ever! Amen." **Revelation 1:4-6**

Below is a quote from our friends over at "GotQuestions.com" concerning the grain offering.

"The grain offering, however, could be somewhat personalized" in its presentation. It was to be given out of a person's free will, just as our worship is our free-will offering to God today. Interestingly, during the Israelites' forty years of wilderness wandering, grain would have been quite scarce. This made grain offerings more costly and precious for the people to offer to God. In those circumstances, giving a grain offering represented the Israelites' complete dependence on God to provide for their needs each day. Jesus fulfilled the Law (**Matthew 5:17**), and we are no longer required to perform sacrifices as they did in the Old Testament. But, if the grain offering is like our offering of worship, it's interesting to consider: How much does our worship today cost us?"

Remember, we have positional faithfulness as the elect of God and provisional faithfulness, which is our walk with the Lord while living on earth.

You say: I don't understand the difference.

Positional security in Christ means all things that we obtain from the Father really belong only to Jesus. Righteousness, sanctification, justification, glorification, faithfulness, hope, blessings, assurance, joy, peace, love, etc.—all of these are given to believers as a byproduct of being in Christ and can never be obtained from the Father any other way. Those are permanent standings with God through the eternal Son, Christ Jesus.

Provisional security in Christ is related to our level of experience with all those things listed above within positional security irrespective of our personnel circumstances. Those who are walking in the Spirit and upright before the Lord can experience great peace amid the worst tempest. While others whine and cry about storm clouds being forecasted for next week. The key is how we are walking.

Now listen to this. This is so awesome. What does the word of God say about how believers are to walk?

1. Walk in the Spirit
   a. "^{16} I say then: Walk in the Spirit, and you shall not fulfill the lust of the flesh." **Galatians 5:16**
2. Walk in good works
   a. "^{10} For we are His workmanship, created in Christ Jesus for good works, which God prepared beforehand that we should walk in them." **Ephesians 2:10**
3. Walk after the Spirit
   a. "^{1}There is therefore now no condemnation to those who are in Christ Jesus, who do not walk according to the flesh, but according to the Spirit." **Romans 8:1**
4. Walk after His commandments
   a. "^{6} This is love, that we walk according to His commandments. This is the commandment, that as you have heard from the beginning, you should walk in it." **2 John 1:6**
5. Walk by faith
   a. "^{7} For we walk by faith, not by sight. ^{8} We are confident, yes, well pleased rather to be absent from the body and to be present with the Lord." **2 Corinthians 5:7-8**

6. Walk in the light
   a. "⁷ But if we walk in the light as He is in the light, we have fellowship with one another, and the blood of Jesus Christ His Son cleanses us from all sin." **1 John 1:7**
7. Walk in wisdom
   a. "⁵ Walk in wisdom toward those who are outside, redeeming the time." **Colossians 4:5**
8. Walk in truth
   a. "⁴ I have no greater joy than to hear that my children walk in truth." **3 John 1:4**
9. Walk in Christ
   a. "⁶ As you therefore have received Christ Jesus the Lord, so walk in Him," **Colossians 2:6**
10. Walk worthy of God
    a. "¹² that you would walk worthy of God who calls you into His own kingdom and glory." **1 Thessalonians 2:12**
11. Walk in honesty
    a. "¹² That you may walk honestly toward those that are outside, and that you may lack of nothing." **1 Thessalonians 4:12**
12. Walk in love
    a. "² And walk in love, as Christ also has loved us and given Himself for us, an offering and a sacrifice to God for a sweet-smelling aroma." **Ephesians 5:2**
13. Walk in God's ways
    a. "³ They also do no iniquity; They walk in His ways." **Psalms 119:3**

Contrast that with the walk of unbelievers who follow their father, the devil.

1. Walk in the ways of darkness
    a. "¹³ From those who leave the paths of uprightness to walk in the ways of darkness;" **Proverbs 2:13**
2. Walk in their own ways
    a. "¹⁶ who in bygone generations allowed all nations to walk in their own ways." **Acts 14:16**
3. Walk in the imagination of their heart and after other gods
    a. "¹⁰ This evil people, who refuse to hear My words, who follow the dictates of their hearts, and walk after other gods to serve them and worship them, shall be just like this sash which is profitable for nothing." **Jeremiah 13:10**
4. Walk in the night
    a. "¹⁰ But if one walks in the night, he stumbles, because the light is not in him." **John 11:10**
5. Walk in darkness
    a. "⁶ If we say that we have fellowship with Him, and walk in darkness, we lie and do not practice the truth." **1 John 1:6**
6. Walk after their own ungodly lusts
    a. "¹⁸ how they told you that there would be mockers in the last time who would walk according to their own ungodly lusts." **Jude 1:18**
7. Walk in the vanity of their mind
    a. "¹⁷ This I say, therefore, and testify in the Lord, that you should no longer walk as the rest of the Gentiles walk,

in the futility of their mind, [18] having their understanding darkened, being alienated from the life of God, because of the ignorance that is in them, because of the blindness of their heart; [19] who, being past feeling, have given themselves over to lewdness, to work all uncleanness with greediness." **Ephesians 4:17-19**

8. Walk after the flesh in the lust of uncleanness
    a. "[10] and especially those who walk according to the flesh in the lust of uncleanness and despise authority. They are presumptuous, self-willed. They are not afraid to speak evil of dignitaries," **2 Peter 2:10**

What a drastic difference between the two groups!

* * *

Now, returning to Hebrews 10, these rebellious actions of deliberately rejecting the Lord are not unique to the New Testament. According to the Mosaic law and statutes, acts of deliberate and premeditated sin received the just penalty enforced by the righteousness of God's laws.

Exclusion from the congregation of Israel; "[29] One and the same law applies to everyone who sins unintentionally, whether a native-born Israelite or a foreigner residing among you. [30] "'But anyone who sins defiantly, whether native-born or foreigner, blasphemes the LORD and must be cut off from the people of Israel. [31] Because they have despised the LORD's word and broken his commands, they must surely be cut off; their guilt remains on them.'" **Numbers 15:29-31**

Exclusion from its worship; [12] "Anyone who strikes a person with a fatal blow is to be put to death. [13] However, if it is not done intentionally, but God lets it happen, they are to flee to a place I will designate. ¹⁴ But if anyone schemes and kills someone deliberately, that person is to be taken from my altar and put to death." **Exodus 21:12-14**

Exclusion from sanctuary in the cities of refuge; "¹¹ But if out of hate someone lies in wait, assaults and kills a neighbor, and then flees to one of these cities, ¹² the killer shall be sent for by the town elders, be brought back from the city, and be handed over to the avenger of blood to die. ¹³ Show no pity. You must purge from Israel the guilt of shedding innocent blood, so that it may go well with you." **Deuteronomy 19:11-13**

This knowledge denotes specific spiritual understanding, not general spiritual knowledge. Yet, the application of the knowledge was flawed like Judas and Alexander the coppersmith. Both became apostates. Apostates are beyond salvation because they have rejected the only sacrifice acceptable to God the Father that can cleanse them from sin and bring them into God's presence. Turning away from the sacrifice of Jesus through the eternal Spirit leaves the apostates with no recourse or salvation alternative. Essentially, these people committed today's unpardonable sin, unbelief.

What is the recourse for dying in an unbelief state? Dying with your sins still residing on you?

Hebrews 10:27 states that there is "A fearful expectation of judgment," which is certain to happen, as God has confirmed His promise to judge the world in righteousness by raising Jesus from the grave. Listen to Paul as he presents the gospel to the Greeks at Athens.

"³⁰ Truly, these times of ignorance God overlooked, but now commands all men everywhere to repent, ³¹ because He has appointed a day on which He will judge the world in righteousness by the Man whom He has ordained. He has given assurance of this to all by raising Him from the dead." **Acts 17:30-31**

After the judgment, it is fiery indignation, in the eternal darkness of the lake of fire that burns with brimstone where the worms never die, the fire is never quenched, where there will be weeping and gnashing of teeth. This judgment is only for those who are adversarial toward God and against the plan of God for salvation. That is to say, all unbelievers.

Hearing this, one may ask: Can it get worse?

It absolutely can and will.

You ask: How so?

God says in Hebrews 10:29, "of how much worse punishment shall there be for those that hear the gospel repeatedly yet rejects Jesus Christ, thereby trampling on the Son of God, counting the blood of the covenant, which is God's only method for positional spiritual sanctification, leading to insulting the Holy Spirit who is testifying to the offering of the grace of God."

Beloved, just as there will be rewards given in heaven based on our faithfulness to maximize our individual gifts distributed by the Holy Spirit, there will also be degrees of punishment in hell. This is also clearly taught in scripture. Those that allow their flesh, the world wicked system, and the demonic hoards influence them the most will have a far worst experience in hell. You can read about these people in Romans chapter 1. Yet that is nothing compared to people that had daily opportunities to hear the word of God, like those of us in America and other free nations, yet still reject God's gift of salvation. How much worse punishment will Americans receive compared to those in Communist and false religious nations who cannot freely hear the word of God. I tremble at that thought.

The following is an extended excerpt for clarity and context.

"[20] Then Jesus began to denounce the towns in which most of his miracles had been performed, because they did not repent. [21] "Woe to you, Chorazin! Woe to you, Bethsaida! For if the miracles that were performed in you had been performed in Tyre and Sidon, they would have repented long ago in sackcloth and ashes. [22] But I tell you, it will be more bearable for Tyre and Sidon on the day of judgment than for you. [23] And you, Capernaum, will you be lifted to the heavens? No, you will go down to Hades. For if the miracles that were performed in you had been performed in Sodom, it would have remained to this day. [24] But I tell you that it will be more bearable for Sodom on the day of judgment than for you." **Matthew 11:20-24**

"[45] But if that servant says in his heart, 'My master is delaying his coming,' and begins to beat the male and female servants, and to eat and drink and be drunk, [46] the master of that servant will come on a day when he is not looking for him, and at an hour when he is not aware, and will cut him in two and appoint him his portion with the unbelievers. [47] And that servant who knew his master's will and did not prepare himself or do according to his will, **shall be beaten with many stripes**. [48] But he who did not know, yet committed things deserving of stripes, **shall be beaten with few**. For everyone to whom much is given, from him much will be required; and to whom much has been committed, of him they will ask the more." **Luke 12:45-48**

Note that both are beaten. Yet, more exposure to the gospel brings a more severe judgment upon the unbeliever.

You may ask: Why?

Because it shows absolute contempt for the sacrifice of Jesus Christ, the Son of God, and for the gift of salvation offered by God the Father, and the witness of the Holy Spirit concerning Christ's redeeming grace. Beloved, God is just and will meet out punishment based upon the works (behavior) and opportunities (exposure to the gospel) of all unbelievers.

CHAPTER 4

THE TORMENT OF II PETER 2

Now, turning to 2 Peter 2. This is a relatively easy chapter to explain; however, we would require far more space than we have in this book to do it justice. I will just provide highlights with enough substance that the meaning will become crystal clear even for a child.

Peter describes the five characteristics of apostate false teachers.

1. Destructive doctrines
2. Distorted doctrine
3. Doom pronounced
4. Depravity
5. Deceptive

Verse 1 is the key, as Peter tells us about whom his comments are directed—false teachers. Therefore, everything that is being said is about false teachers.
You ask: What about them?

Notice the first thing Peter identifies, the **destructive** doctrines. They use subtlety to deceive people in the church then secretly bring in destructive false doctrine even to the point where they deny the deity of Christ.

The deity of Christ?

Yes, that Jesus Christ was, is, and always will be, God and there is none other besides Him.

Peter says that they will deceive many, which will lead to immoral behavior, thereby bringing disrepute on the word of God and upon the church. They will refuse to preach about repentance, sin, or holiness.

Do you know any preachers like that today?

I do.

"[1] But there were also false prophets among the people, just as there will be false teachers among you. They will secretly introduce destructive heresies, even denying the sovereign Lord who bought them, bringing swift destruction on themselves. [2] Many will follow their depraved conduct and will bring the way of truth into disrepute" **2 Peter 2:1-2**

The second thing that Peter stated these false teachers did, was bring **distorted** doctrine into the church, the prosperity gospel. Peter said that they will fleece the flock of God. The false teachers will tell people that God wants them to be the head and not the tail, that they have the authority to decree something into existence, and if they can just muster up enough faith, they can and will be healed or pray that someone else will be healed. They will have the people giving their house note, light bill, and grocery money while they caravan around in $200k cars, multimillion-dollar homes, and private jets. These wolves are just like the

Pharisees who had the widow under so much guilt that she gave up her last two mites to then go home and die.

How many times did God condemn Israel for such wicked conduct against the poor, orphans, and widows? Do a biblical word search on "poor", "orphan", and "widow" to see the compassion that God has for them. Then visit one of these megachurches to see how the leadership lives. I tell you, it makes the Lord sick. Where is their compassion for the poor, orphans, and widows? The church spends more on coffee, snacks, and entertainment than helping the family whose father just lost his job and currently have little to no means to provide for his family. They say to him, "Oh brother, we are praying for you", then quickly run to a restaurant where a meal for two cost them $150. Then drive to the airport to board one of their private jets where the standby pilot and jet fuel for a weekend trip to a "religious retreat" will cost more than most of their members' homes. How tragic and disgusting. In the day of visitation, when the judgment of the Lord is meted out in the vengeance of His wrath, these apostate preachers will receive their just reward.

"[14] The LORD will enter into judgment with the elders of His people And His princes:

"For you have eaten up the vineyard; The plunder of the poor is in your houses. [15] What do you mean by crushing My people and grinding the faces of the poor?" Says the Lord GOD of hosts." **Isaiah 3:14-15**

"[1] "Woe to those who decree unrighteous decrees, who write misfortune, which they have prescribed [2] To rob the needy of justice, and to take what is right from the poor of My people, that widows may be their prey, and that they may rob the fatherless. ³ What will you do in the day of punishment, and in the desolation which will come from afar? To whom will you flee for help? and where will you leave your glory? ⁴ Without Me they shall bow down among the prisoners, and they shall fall among the slain." For all this His anger is not turned away, But His hand is stretched out still." **Isaiah 10:1-4**

The Lord God will rescue the poor, orphans, and widows from the mouth of these ravenous wolves.

"¹ O LORD, You are my God. I will exalt You, I will praise Your name, For You have done wonderful things; Your counsels of old are faithfulness and truth. ⁴ For You have been a strength to the poor, A strength to the needy in his distress, A refuge from the storm,

A shade from the heat;" **Isaiah 25:1-4**

"¹⁷ "The poor and needy seek water, but there is none, their tongues fail for thirst.

I, the LORD, will hear them; I, the God of Israel, will not forsake them." **Isaiah 41:17**

*   *   *

Now back to 2 Peter 2. The Lord said that these false teachers will face His wrath for their greed and fleecing His flock.

"³ In their greed these teachers will exploit you with fabricated stories. Their condemnation has long been hanging over them, and their destruction has not been sleeping." **2 Peter 2:3**

These men will attempt to rule over the people by stating that they have special revelations from God. When you hear someone say that, run away as fast as you can. The Canon of Scripture is closed. God has spoken to us in these last days through His Son.

"[1] In the past God spoke to our ancestors through the prophets at many times and in various ways, [2] but in these last days he has spoken to us by his Son, whom he appointed heir of all things, and through whom also he made the universe." **Hebrews 1:1-2**

If the Lord Jesus shows up at your house, entering through the wall and telling you something that is not in the Bible, kick him out. Peter said that the Bible is a more sure word than his, James', and John's eyewitness accounts at the mount of transfiguration.

"[19] And so we have the prophetic word confirmed, which you do well to heed as a light that shines in a dark place, until the day dawns and the morning star rises in your hearts;" **2 Peter 1:19**

All we need today is the Bible and the Holy Spirit. We are to follow pastors and teachers who are anointed and appointed by God only if they are following Christ and teaching the word of God. How in the world would you know that they are teaching the word of God if you are not reading your Bible? Put the stupid phone and tablet down! Delete the time-wasting social media apps! Turn off the garbagevision! Then dedicate that time to studying the word of God.

Third, Peter declares the **doom** of the false teachers from verses 4 through 11 by way of examples.

1. From heaven—the fallen angels—kicked out of heaven with some locked in the abyss in chains
2. To men—the flood—drowned millions, maybe even billions, men-women-children

3. To cities and nations —Sodom, Gomorrah, and surrounding area—fire and brimstone rained down from heaven

God distinguishes between believers and unbelievers by sparing the holy angels, delivering Noah's family, and Lot's family, but none of the ungodly escaped judgment, nor will the false teachers. This, beloved, is the preservation of the saints. This is why a believer can never be lost. Peter said believers are kept saved by the power of God, not by our works.

"³ Blessed be the God and Father of our Lord Jesus Christ, who according to His abundant mercy has begotten us again to a living hope through the resurrection of Jesus Christ from the dead, ⁴ to an inheritance incorruptible and undefiled and that does not fade away, reserved in heaven for you, ⁵ who are kept by the power of God through faith for salvation ready to be revealed in the last time." **1 Peter 1:3-5**

Jude declared that God our Savior, the Lord Jesus Christ, keeps us from stumbling and will present us to the Father without faults with exceeding joy.

"²⁴ Now to Him who is able to keep you from stumbling, and to present you faultless before the presence of His glory with exceeding joy, ²⁵ To God our Savior, who alone is wise, be glory and majesty, dominion, and power, both now and forever. Amen." **Jude 1:24-25**

Paul pronounced through the Holy Spirit, that nothing can separate us from God, ever.

"³⁷ Yet in all these things we are more than conquerors through Him who loved us. ³⁸ For I am persuaded that neither death nor life, nor angels nor principalities nor powers, nor things present nor things to come, ³⁹ nor height nor depth, **nor any other created thing**, shall be able to separate us from the love of God which is in Christ Jesus our Lord." **Romans 8:37-39**

Paul also stated that we can depend upon the Lord's faithfulness.

"⁶ God thus confirming our testimony about Christ among you. ⁷ Therefore you do not lack any spiritual gift as you eagerly wait for our Lord Jesus Christ to be revealed. ⁸ **He will also keep you firm to the end, so that you will be blameless on the day of our Lord Jesus Christ.** ⁹ **God is faithful,** who has called you into fellowship with his Son, Jesus Christ our Lord." **1 Corinthians 1:6-9**

Finally, our great God and Savior, who is the final word declared that no one can remove a true believer, his sheep, from his hand, for there is none greater.

"²⁷ My sheep listen to my voice; I know them, and they follow me. ²⁸ I give them eternal life, and they shall never perish; no one will snatch them out of my hand. ²⁹ My Father, who has given them to me, is greater than all; no one can snatch them out of my Father's hand. ³⁰ I and the Father are one." **John 10:27-30**

I cannot speak on your behalf, beloved, but Kevin can never and will never be lost.

You say: "how can you be so confident in yourself?"

Beloved, I have absolutely no confidence in myself, but I, like Paul, am fully persuaded in our Lord's ability to keep me according to His word.

"[12] For this reason I also suffer these things; nevertheless, I am not ashamed, for I know whom I have believed and am persuaded that He is able to keep what I have committed to Him until that Day." **2 Timothy 1:12**

Listen to our God and Savior prayer to our Father. Extended excerpt for context and clarity.

"[9] "I pray for them. I do not pray for the world but for those whom You have given Me, for they are Yours. [10] And all Mine are Yours, and Yours are Mine, and I am glorified in them. [11] Now I am no longer in the world, but these are in the world, and I come to You. Holy Father, keep through Your name those whom You have given Me, that they may be one as We are. [12] While I was with them in the world, I kept them in Your name. Those whom You gave Me I have kept; and **none of them is lost** except the son of perdition, that the Scripture might be fulfilled..."[20] "**I do not pray for these alone, but also for those who will believe in Me through their word;** [21] **that they all may be one**, as You, Father, are in Me, and I in You; that they also may be one in Us, that the world may believe that You sent Me. [22] And the glory which You gave Me I have given them, that they may be one just as We are one: [23] I in them, and You in Me; that they may be made perfect in one, and that the world may know that You have sent Me, and have loved them as You have loved Me." **John 17:9-12, 20-23**

All glory, honor, and praise be unto You, O Lord GOD almighty for Your amazing grace. I stand in awe of You and bow to worship before Your throne, for You are holy. Amen.

I still have difficulty believing Lot was saved, but God through Peter testified that Lot was righteous, meaning he was a true believer.

"⁷ and delivered righteous Lot, who was oppressed by the filthy conduct of the wicked ⁸ (for that righteous man, dwelling among them, tormented his righteous soul from day to day by seeing and hearing their lawless deeds) ⁹ then the Lord knows how to deliver the godly out of temptations and to reserve the unjust under punishment for the day of judgment," **2 Peter 2:7-9**

* * *

Okay, back to 2 Peter 2. Note that God points out those who have the most egregious behavior for the worst punishment.

"¹⁰ and especially those who walk according to the flesh in the lust of uncleanness and despise authority. They are presumptuous, self-willed. They are not afraid to speak evil of dignitaries," **2 Peter 2:10**

Let me point to a couple of verses that fit here perfectly but are often overlooked. We often wonder why the Lord delays judgment. However, there a several references regarding the longsuffering of God that we just cannot comprehend.

"²⁴ The sins of some are obvious, reaching the place of judgment ahead of them; the sins of others trail behind them. ²⁵ In the same way, good deeds are obvious, and even those that are not obvious cannot remain hidden forever." **1 Timothy 5:24-25**

Do you understand the principle the Spirit of God describing in this verse?

Although the context is concerning the office of elders in the church, the principle applies to the judgment. He is saying that the thief, murderer, sexual deviant, etc., who is rejoicing over not being caught here on earth will pay in full on judgment day. Likewise, those of us that no one knows or are aware of our obedience and faithfulness to the ministry placed upon us by the Lord will be rewarded in heaven. By ministry, I do not mean serving in a building but raising godly children, feeding the poor, taking care of the elderly and widows, taking care of our elderly parents. These things go unnoticed by the church however they are gold, silver, and precious stones to our God and King.

"8 But, beloved, do not forget this one thing, that with the Lord one day is as a thousand years, and a thousand years as one day. 9 The Lord is not slack concerning His promise, as some count slackness, but is longsuffering toward us, not willing that any should perish but that all should come to repentance." **2 Peter 3:8-9**

God is patient but one day that patience will run out and the rain of God's judgment will fall.

Fourth, Peter identifies the **depravity** of false teachers.

"12 But these, like natural brute beasts made to be caught and destroyed, speak evil of the things they do not understand, and will utterly perish in their own corruption, 13 and will receive the wages of unrighteousness, as those who count it pleasure to carouse in the daytime. They are spots and blemishes, carousing in their own deceptions while they feast with you, 14 having eyes full of adultery and that cannot cease from sin, enticing unstable souls. They have a heart trained in covetous practices and are accursed children. 15 They have forsaken the right way and gone astray, following the way of Balaam the son of Beor, who loved the wages of unrighteousness; 16 but he was rebuked for his iniquity: a dumb donkey speaking with a man's voice restrained the madness of the prophet.17 These are wells without water, clouds carried by a tempest, for whom is reserved the blackness of darkness forever." **2 Peter 2:12-17**

These false teachers are brute beasts, meaning they have no sensitivity to spiritual matters. They discount the power and presence of demons or holy angels, but like wild animals, recalcitrant, impudent, and egotistical, they charge into the supernatural realm, declaring and rebuking away at persons and spiritual matters they do not understand. There is no scriptural basis for believers to so-call rebuke the devil. Even the leader of the Lord's heavenly army, Michael the archangel, would not rebuke Satan as the devil outranks him. Michael calls on the Lord to rebuke Satan. We wonder why these types of prayers are never answered.

Since they live like brute beasts, the false teachers will be killed like brute beasts, ensnared in their own folly. False teachers cannot get beyond their own instincts, and thus, will be destroyed by the recklessness of their passions.

1. Wages of unrighteousness—speaks of their secretive immorality and arrogance
2. Carouse in the daytime—most sinners wait for the cover of darkness, but these are so deceptive and deceitful that they play in plain sight during the day. Even when it is obvious to most, their flock has been blinded by the devil. Think Jim Jones and others like him.
3. Spots and blemishes—God calls them sore scabs; their character is the opposite of Christ and the true Church.
   a. "[19]but with the precious blood of Christ, as of a lamb without blemish and without spot" **1 Peter 1:19**
4. Eyes full of adultery—no self-control and full of lustful thoughts

5. Enticing unstable souls—they use fishing bait; they do not capture those who are strong in the Word but seek out the feeble, insecure, and babes in Christ.
6. Heart trained in covetous practices—they only seek self-fulfillment and not Christ; they are earth dwellers that mind only earthly things.
7. Like Balaam—a prophet for hire. They are a hireling
   a. "¹² But a hireling, he who is not the shepherd, one who does not own the sheep, sees the wolf coming and leaves the sheep and flees; and the wolf catches the sheep and scatters them. ¹³ The hireling flees because he is a hireling and does not care about the sheep." **John 10:12-13**
8. Wells without water—the word of God does not dwell within them richly. Therefore, they cannot wash the feet of the sheep.
9. Clouds carried by a tempest—they only show the promise of life-giving rain, only to provide a passing shade that can never bring satisfaction and nourishment that lead to growth.
   a. "³ If you walk in My statutes and keep My commandments, and perform them, ⁴ then I will give you rain in its season, the land shall yield its produce, and the trees of the field shall yield their fruit." **Leviticus 26:3-4**

Fifth, Peter describes the **deceptions** of false teachers.

"¹⁸ For when they speak great swelling words of emptiness, they allure through the lusts of the flesh, through lewdness, the ones who have actually escaped from those who live in error. ¹⁹ While they promise them liberty, they themselves are slaves of corruption; for by whom a person is overcome, by him also he is brought into bondage. [20] For if, after they have escaped the pollutions of the world through the knowledge of the Lord and Savior Jesus Christ, they are again entangled in them and overcome, the latter end is worse for them than the beginning. [21] For it would have been better for them not to have known the way of righteousness, than having known it, to turn from the holy commandment delivered to them. [22] But it has happened to them according to the true proverb: "A dog returns to his own vomit," and, "a sow, having washed, to her wallowing in the mire." **2 Peter 2:18-22**

1. Great swelling words—great orators of empty words, which deceives the weak and gullible. If you listen to them carefully, you can have your best life now here on earth instead of in the New Jerusalem with the Holy One of Israel, the Lord Jesus Christ.

   It absolutely befuddles me how anyone can have their best life now in a wicked world. Eat, drink, and be merry for tomorrow we die. Listen to what the Lord said to people desiring their best life now.

   "[16] Then He spoke a parable to them, saying: "The ground of a certain rich man yielded plentifully. [17] And he thought within himself, saying, 'What shall I do, since I have no room to store my crops?' [18] So he said, 'I will do this: I will pull down my barns and build greater, and there I will store all my crops and my goods. [19] And I will say to my soul, "Soul, you have many goods laid up for many years; take your ease; eat, drink, and be merry."' [20] But God said to him, 'Fool! This night your soul will be required of you; then whose will those things be which you have provided?' ²¹ "So is he who lays up treasure for himself, and is not rich toward God." **Luke 12:16-21**

Is there anything in this life now that can compared to beholding the glory of our great God and Savior face to face and worshipping before His holy throne? Will we ever witness life here on earth compared to this:

"¹ Now I saw a new heaven and a new earth, for the first heaven and the first earth had passed away. Also there was no more sea. ² Then I, John, saw the holy city, New Jerusalem, coming down out of heaven from God, prepared as a bride adorned for her husband. ³ And I heard a loud voice from heaven saying, "Behold, the tabernacle of God is with men, and He will dwell with them, and they shall be His people. God Himself will be with them and be their God. ⁴ And God will wipe away every tear from their eyes; there shall be no more death, nor sorrow, nor crying. There shall be no more pain, for the former things have passed away." **Revelation 21:1-4**

May the Lord have mercy upon these deceivers and deliver them from their blindness bringing them to the knowledge of truth through true faith in His Son.

2. Allure to the flesh—they appeal to the natural man who seeks after earthly things instead of setting their affections on things above because they are disinterested in heavenly things.

3. Actually escaped—they ensnare natural people in their nets through their vulnerabilities: hopes, dreams, disappointments, loneliness, religion, hopelessness, desire for riches.

4. Promise liberty—this is what keeps people coming back; it is like playing the lottery.
5. Slaves of corruption—they cannot give something they do not possess; Jesus described them as whitewashed tombs full of dead men bones. Corruption in the word of God represent sin. Paul said, "[16] Do you not know that to whom you present yourselves slaves to obey, you are that one's slaves whom you obey, whether of sin leading to death, or of obedience leading to righteousness?" **Romans 6:16**

And of course, they don't know because being a child of the devil, he uses them whenever he chooses.

6. Bondage—instead of providing freedom, the people become the meal.
7. Escape pollutions—this represents the smell from the corruption of sin in the human heart. They put lipstick and perfume on a corpse. One can never escape the corruption of sin by an outward change of behavior, training the flesh to be religious. I will repeat it again, saying a prayer cannot save anyone, attending church cannot save anyone, reading the Bible cannot save anyone, being a moral person cannot save anyone. Salvation is of the Lord, who calls through grace, provide saving faith as a gift, then regenerates (create a new spirit) the spirit within our human body. This new spirit possessed by the Holy Spirit then begins to manifest the new person through a change in outward behavior. This process is called the new birth or being born again from above.
8. Turn from the holy commandment—this describes the distortion and defection of the false teachers. They

professed the way of righteousness and even preach from the Bible, but their lives demonstrate rejection of Christ.

    a. "¹⁵ To the pure all things are pure, but to those who are defiled and unbelieving nothing is pure; but even their mind and conscience are defiled. ¹⁶ They profess to know God, but in works they deny Him, being abominable, disobedient, and disqualified for every good work." **Titus 1:15-16**

Although their behavior shows works of righteousness, it is coming from a corrupt heart and mind, therefore in God's eyes their works of righteousness is filthy and an abomination to His holiness.

9. Dog and sow—the false teacher will always be a dog and pig at heart and never a child of God. Note that in 2 Peter 3:1 that Peter begins to address the beloved, the true believers.

"¹ Beloved, I now write to you" **2 Peter 3:1**

Nowhere in the Word of God does the Lord ever address His children as rebels, or dogs, or pigs, or unclean. The reason is simple. If they were deemed any of those things, then God, being holy and righteous, must deal with them in wrath since rebels, dogs, pigs, and unclean people are designated by the scriptures as unbelievers or apostates. Since believers are the body of Christ, with Jesus being the head, God would have to pour out his wrath upon Jesus billions of times daily, every time a believer sins. The book of Hebrews addresses this very issue: extended excerpt for context and clarity.

"Therefore, when Christ came into the world, he said: "Sacrifice and offering you (God the Father) did not desire, but a body you prepared for me; with burnt offerings and sin offerings you were not pleased. Then I said, 'Here I am—it is written about me in the scroll (Old Testament scriptures), I have come to do your will, my God.'" First he said, "Sacrifices and offerings, burnt offerings and sin offerings you did not desire, **nor were you pleased with them**" though they were offered in accordance with the law. Then he said, "Here I am, I have come to do your will." He sets aside the first (the law through works) to establish the second (the new covenant of grace through faith). And by that will (God's grace through faith), we have been **made holy** (by the Father) through the sacrifice of the body of Jesus Christ (not by works) **once (forever) for all (for everyone that believe)**. Day after day every priest stands and performs his **religious duties (that's us without Christ)**; again and again he offers the same sacrifices, **which can never take away sins. (this is the entire issue, what can take away my sins and your sins?)** But when this priest (Jesus) had offered **for all time (forever) one sacrifice** (never to be repeated) **for sins (only Christ sacrifice can take away sins)**, he sat down at the right hand of God (Jesus' work of offering himself for sins forever, was completed and accepted by God), and since that time he waits for his enemies to be made his footstool. For by one sacrifice (the cross), he (Jesus) **has made perfect forever (positional** justification, sanctification, and glorification) those **who are being made holy (provisional** sanctification while we are walking on the earth, where our feet get dirty and requires confession of sins and washing by the Holy Spirit**)**.

The Holy Spirit also testifies to us about this. First, he (the Holy Spirit is God) says, "This is the covenant I will make with them (anyone that believes in Jesus) after that time, says the Lord. I will put my laws in their hearts (our new spirit), and I will write them on their minds." Then he adds, "Their sins and lawless acts I will remember no more. (never ever)" and where these (sins: past, present, and future) have been forgiven (they were forgiven over 2,000 years ago on the cross), sacrifice for sin is no longer necessary (because they no longer exist in the eyes and mind of God)." **Hebrews 10:5-18**

Paul listed the ten behavior patterns of an unbeliever; "do you not know that the unrighteous will not inherit the kingdom of God? **Do not be [1]deceived**: Neither the [2]**sexually immoral,** nor [3]**idolaters,** nor [4]**adulterers,** nor [5]**homosexuals,** nor [6]**thieves,** nor [7]**the materialistic,** nor [8]**drunkards,** nor [9]**slanderers,** nor [10]**swindlers,** will inherit the kingdom of God. That is what **some of you were!**

He then went on to say about the believers, "but you are **washed**, but you are **sanctified**, but you are **justified…**" **1 Cor. 6:9-11a**

How Paul? I'm glad you asked. By faith "…in the name of the Lord Jesus, and by the Spirit of our God." **V11b**

John, through the Spirit of God, said this about true believers, "[4] Everyone who sins breaks the law; in fact, sin is lawlessness. [5] But you know that he appeared so that he might take away our sins. **And in him (Christ) is no sin** (all believers are in Christ). [6] **No one who lives in him keeps on sinning. No one who continues to sin has either seen him or known him.**

[7] Dear children, do not let anyone lead you astray. The one who does what is right is righteous, just as he is righteous. [8] The one who does what is sinful is of the devil, because the devil has been sinning from the beginning. The reason the Son of God appeared was to destroy the devil's work. [9] **No one who is born of God**

will continue to sin, (Why not Lord?) Because God's seed (the Holy Spirit) remains in them; they **cannot** go on sinning, because they have been born of God." **1 John 3:4-9**

The Holy Spirit will not allow God's children to persist in sins.

Oh, beloved, please do not miss this great truth. The reason we are none of these things, rebels, dogs, hogs, unclean, sexually immoral, idolaters, adulterers, etc., is because of Him! Outside of Christ, we are wretched, filthy, rotten sinners. The only reason the Father would ever look our way is because of Jesus.

"[57] But thanks be to God, who gives us the victory through our Lord Jesus Christ. [58] Therefore, my beloved brethren, be steadfast, immovable, always abounding in the work of the Lord, knowing that your labor is not in vain in the Lord." **1 Corinthians 15:57-58**

We are in this race together. Keep running, beloved. Do not be afraid. The Lord God is our sword and shield, and our exceedingly great reward.

"[1] The LORD is my light and my salvation; Whom shall I fear? The LORD is the strength of my life; of whom shall I be afraid? [2] When the wicked came against me to eat up my flesh, My enemies and foes, they stumbled and fell. [3] Though an army may encamp against me, my heart shall not fear; Though war may rise against me, in this I will be confident. [4] One thing I have desired of the LORD, that will I seek: That I may dwell in the house of the LORD all the days of my life, to behold the beauty of the LORD, and to inquire in His temple. [5] For in the time of trouble He shall hide me in His pavilion; In the secret place of His tabernacle, He shall hide me; He shall set me high upon a rock." **Psalms 27:1-5**

Look up, beloved. Our redemption draws near!

I will praise you, O Lord, with all my heart. I will lift my voice and sing praises to Your glorious Name, for You alone are holy. To You, O Lord, belong the power, glory, majesty, and dominion. Your kingdom, Father, is an everlasting kingdom, and Your dominion shall never end. One generation shall praise Your name to another, and all Your saints shall worship before Your throne. For You are the great, the mighty, the awesome, the terrible God, the Lord of hosts is Your name!

PART 4

THE FINAL LINK IN THE CHAIN

CHAPTER 1

JESUS' INSPECTS HIS BODY

The Book of Revelation is God's final record of His plans to remove all impurities from creation. The record presents a synopsis of the redemptive plan of God. It reveals the divine nature of the Lord Jesus Christ and how the holy name of the Most High God is vindicated before all creation. Although each book of the Bible contains prophecies or reveals the redeeming nature of God, Revelation is the only New Testament book that focuses primarily on prophetic events. Revelation means "an unveiling," "a disclosure," "an announcement," or "a declaration," all befitting descriptions for the glorious unfurling of the plan of God. Revelation put on display the true personality, disposition, and program of the Father.

Throughout the New Testament, we see the word "revelation" utilized to describe the unveiling of spiritual truth.

"^{25} Now to Him who is able to establish you according to my gospel and the preaching of Jesus Christ, according to the revelation of the mystery kept secret since the world began ^{26} but now made manifest, and by the prophetic Scriptures made known to all nations, according to the commandment of the everlasting God, for obedience to the faith ^{27} to God, alone wise, be glory through Jesus Christ forever. Amen." **Romans 16:25-27**

The temporary setting aside of His people Israel to purchase a bride for His Son. Not only is this revealed in the New Testament, but it was prophesied in the Old Testament by several of the prophets, including Isaiah.

"^{25} For I do not desire, brethren, that you should be ignorant of this mystery, lest you should be wise in your own opinion, that blindness in part has happened to Israel until the fullness of the Gentiles has come in. ^{26} And so all Israel will be saved, as it is written: "The Deliverer will come out of Zion, and He will turn away ungodliness from Jacob; ^{27} For this is My covenant with them, When I take away their sins." **Romans 11:25-27**

The Father's love gift to His Son, the selection of the bride of Christ, members of the Church. Only those who are called, chosen, and elected will hear the effectual calling of the Father.

Who are these called, chosen, and elected people?

All those who repent of their sins and believe in Jesus as Lord, Savior, and King. They are the whosoever will let them come group. Repentance in this sense means a recognition of our helpless and hopeless sinful condition, understanding that only Jesus can deliver and save.

"^{3} how that by revelation **He made known to me the mystery** (as I have briefly written already, ^{4} by which, when you read, you may understand my knowledge in the mystery of Christ), ^{5} **which in other ages** was not made known to the sons of men, as it has now been revealed by the Spirit to His holy apostles and prophets: ^{6} that the Gentiles should be fellow heirs, of the same body, and partakers of His promise in Christ through the gospel," **Ephesians 3:3-6**

The gospel revealed.

"¹⁶ Beyond all question, **the mystery** from which true godliness springs is great: God appeared in the flesh, was vindicated by the Spirit, was seen by angels, was preached among the nations, was believed on in the world, was taken up in glory." **1 Timothy 3:16**

The incarnation of Jesus the Christ.

²⁹ "Lord, now You are letting Your servant depart in peace, according to Your word; ³⁰ For my eyes have seen Your salvation ³¹ Which You have prepared **before the face of all peoples**, ³² A light to bring revelation to the Gentiles, and the glory of Your people Israel." **Luke 2:29-32**

The glory of the Cross.

"⁶ However, we speak wisdom among those who are mature, yet not the wisdom of this age, nor of the rulers of this age, who are coming to nothing. ⁷ But we speak **the wisdom of God in a mystery**, the hidden wisdom which God ordained before the ages for our glory, ⁸ which none of the rulers of this age knew; for had they known, they would not have crucified the Lord of glory." **1 Corinthians 2:6-8**

The birth of the Church.

"²⁵ Now to Him who is able to establish you according to my gospel and the preaching of Jesus Christ, according to the **revelation of the mystery kept secret since the world began ²⁶ but now made manifest**, and by the prophetic Scriptures made known to all nations, according to the commandment of the everlasting God, for obedience to the faith ²⁷ to God, alone wise, be glory through Jesus Christ forever. Amen." **Romans 16:25-27**

The indwelling presence of Christ in every believer.

"²⁶ **the mystery which has been hidden from ages and from generations**, but now has been revealed to His saints. ²⁷ To them God willed to make known what are the riches of the glory of this mystery among the Gentiles: which is Christ in you, the hope of glory." **Colossians 1:26-27**

The Bridegroom's fellowship with His Beloved, the Church.

"² My goal is that they (the Church) may be encouraged in heart and united in love, so that they may have the full riches of complete understanding, in order **that they may know the mystery of God, namely, Christ,** ³ in whom are hidden all the treasures of wisdom and knowledge." **Colossians 2:2-3**

The Bridegroom's courtship of His Beloved, the Church.

"²⁵ Husbands, love your wives, just as Christ loved the church and gave himself up for her ²⁶ to make her holy, cleansing her by the washing with water through the word, ²⁷ and to present her to himself as a radiant church, without stain or wrinkle or any other blemish, but holy and blameless. ²⁸ In this same way, husbands ought to love their wives as their own bodies. He who loves his wife loves himself. ²⁹ After all, no one ever hated their own body, but they feed and care for their body, just as Christ does the church— ³⁰ for we are members of his body. ³¹ "For this reason a man will leave his father and mother and be united to his wife, and the two will become one flesh." ³² **This is a profound mystery—but I am talking about Christ and the church**. ³³ However, each one of you also must love his wife as he loves himself, and the wife must respect her husband." **Ephesians 5:25-33**

Finally, the revealing of the children of God and bride of Christ to the world at the wedding feast during the Millennium.

"¹⁸ For I consider that the sufferings of this present time are not worthy to be compared with the glory which shall be revealed in us. ¹⁹ For the **earnest expectation of the creation eagerly waits for the revealing of the sons of God.**" **Romans 8:18-19**

In Revelation, the mystery of God in its final consummation of all things answers the prayers of His saints from Adam through the tribulation saints. This includes the prayer given by His Son and prayed billions of times by the Church: Thy Kingdom come, Thy will be done, in earth as it is in heaven. Oh Beloved, do not miss this great truth, the Lord God collects every prayer of His saints. None are lost, and none go unanswered.

You may say: But I do not see the manifestation of my petition?

Allow me to take you on a journey back to the Tabernacle of the Lord. In Exodus 30:1-6, we read the instructions given by the Lord to build the Altar of Incense. This alter was made of acacia wood and overlaid with gold with horns on each corner. It had four gold rings through which two poles made of acacia wood overlaid with gold were used to transport the altar by the priests. The altar was placed before the veil that was before the Ark of the Covenant, directly in front of the mercy seat, which represented the throne of the Lord and His presence above the Ark between the two Cherubins.

Instructions were also given that the priests were to make a special incense as directed by the Lord to burn upon the altar continually. However, only coals from the brazen altar could be utilized to kindle the fire. The High Priest was instructed to make an atonement upon the altar's horns once each year with the blood of the sin offering of atonement as the burning of the incense was most holy to the Lord.

You may ask: Now what does that have to do with Revelation and prayers of the saints never going unanswered?

I'll give you the short version. Ready? The altar seated before the throne of the Father represents Christ, wood for His humanity and gold for divinity. He is the Godman. As our High Priest, Jesus stands before the throne of the Father, making intercession for the Church. Note that the priest was instructed never to offer strange incense upon the altar because the High Priest presenting this offering unto the Lord was the only begotten of the Father and was declared a priest forever.

"[20] And inasmuch as He was not made priest without an oath [21] (for they have become priests without an oath, but He with an oath by Him who said to Him: "The LORD has sworn and will not relent, 'You are a priest forever According to the order of Melchizedek'"), [22] by so much more Jesus has become a surety of a better covenant. [23] Also there were many priests, because they were prevented by death from continuing. [24] But He, because He continues forever, has an unchangeable priesthood. [25] Therefore He is also able to save to the uttermost those who come to God through Him, since He always lives to make intercession for them. [26] For such a High Priest was fitting for us, who is holy, harmless, undefiled, separate from sinners, and has become higher than the heavens; [27] who does not need daily, as those high priests, to offer up sacrifices, first for His own sins and then for the people's, for this He did once for all when He offered up Himself. [28] For the law appoints as high priests men who have weakness, but the word of the oath, which came after the law, appoints the Son who has been perfected forever." **Hebrews 7:20-28**

Also, note that Aaron was instructed to make atonement once a year for the Altar of Incense, which when offered by the priests, represented the prayer of the people. Due to the imperfection of the people, it was necessary that the blood of Christ be applied along with the purifying refining fire of the coals from the brazen altar, which represented the propitiating work of the cross. Beloved, even our prayers are unclean to a holy God.

We see this when Zacharias went into the Holy Place to offer incense, and the angel Gabriel announced that John the Baptist would be born. While he burned the incense, all the people stood without the tabernacle praying.

"[8] So it was, that while he was serving as priest before God in the order of his division, [9] according to the custom of the priesthood, his lot fell to burn incense when he went into the temple of the Lord. [10] And the whole multitude of the people was praying outside at the hour of incense. [11] Then an angel of the Lord appeared to him, standing on the right side of the altar of incense. [12] And when Zacharias saw him, he was troubled, and fear fell upon him." **Luke 1:8-12**

Today, the prayers of the saints are offered to the Father by the Holy Spirit through the body of His Son, the Church.

"[26] Likewise the Spirit also helps in our weaknesses. For we do not know what we should pray for as we ought, but the Spirit Himself makes intercession for us with groanings which cannot be uttered. [27] Now He who searches the hearts knows what the mind of the Spirit is, because He makes intercession for the saints according to the will of God." **Romans 8:26-27**

Again, I'll remind you that only the pure special incense can be burned upon this altar, which means that the prayer must be uttered by someone who has no sin and the offering given by someone who has no sin. We, even as redeemed children of God, fail on both accounts. Therefore, we could never offer prayers directly to the Father. Without the intercession of the Holy Spirit and our Lord Jesus Christ, our prayers would fall from our lips to the ground. Praise be to God that our prayers are not only offered before the throne but ascend before Him as a sweet-smelling fragrance. So, how does the Father react when our prayers rise before Him, and what does He do with them?

We find the answer in Revelations 5:4-10.

"⁴ So I wept much, because no one was found worthy to open and read the scroll, or to look at it. ⁵ But one of the elders said to me, "Do not weep. Behold, the Lion of the tribe of Judah, the Root of David, has prevailed to open the scroll and to loose its seven seals." ⁶ And I looked, and behold, in the midst of the throne and of the four living creatures, and in the midst of the elders, stood a Lamb as though it had been slain, having seven horns and seven eyes, which are the seven Spirits of God sent out into all the earth. ⁷ Then He came and took the scroll out of the right hand of Him who sat on the throne. ⁸ Now when He had taken the scroll, the four living creatures and the twenty-four elders fell down before the Lamb, **each having a harp, and golden bowls full of incense, which are the prayers of the saints**. ⁹ And they sang a new song, saying: "You are worthy to take the scroll, And to open its seals; For You were slain, And have redeemed us to God by Your blood Out of every tribe and tongue and people and nation, ¹⁰ And have made us kings and priests to our God;

And we shall reign on the earth." **Revelation 5:4-10**

This is the scene in heaven while the people on the earth are travailing through the seven-year tribulation. The twenty-four elders represent the order of priests for the church. This was the order of priests established by David prior to handing the kingdom to Solomon as a rotation for the service of the temple that Solomon would build (1 Chron. 23).

In verse 8, each of the elders had in their hands golden bowls full of incense, which are the prayers of the saints.

You say: I thought you said that only the Holy Spirit could offer prayers for the Church?

I did not say that. God did. Nevertheless, that was the will of the Father while the Church was on earth living in their unholy fleshly body which Paul called the body of sin. The Church has now been raptured into heaven as depicted in Revelations 4:1 after John delivered the messages from the Lord Jesus to the seven churches in Asia Minor which is modern day Turkey.

"[1] After these things I looked, and behold, **a door standing open in heaven**. And the first voice which I heard was like a trumpet speaking with me, saying, "**Come up here**, and I will show you things which must take place after this." [2] Immediately I was in the Spirit; and behold, a throne set in heaven, and One sat on the throne." **Revelation 4:1-2**

Now in heaven clothed with their glorious body and in perfect unity with the Lord God, the Church can offer prayer directly to the Father and the Lamb, Christ Jesus the Lord. Our motives are now pure and all that we think, say, and do is absolutely aligned with the perfect will of God. Hence, there is no further need for the mediation of the Holy Spirit between the Holy Father and us. The elders have in their possession every prayer ever offered to the Father by every saint that ever walked the earth, and those that we thought went unanswered will soon be in the form of holy wrath upon the rebellious earth-dwellers and the demonic hoard. What is revealed to us in this passage is our patient and longsuffering God. His patience allows time for sinners to repent, but when the fullness of time comes, His perfect justice will be meted upon the unbelievers, the kingdom of the antichrist, and the kingdom of darkness.

Now, notice what happens when the Lamb opens the fifth seal.

"[9] When He opened the fifth seal, I saw under the altar the souls of those who had been slain for the word of God and for the testimony which they held. [10] And they cried with a loud voice, saying, "How long, O Lord, holy and true, until You judge and avenge our blood on those who dwell on the earth?" [11] Then a white robe was given to each of them; and it was said to them that they should rest a little while longer, until both the number of their fellow servants and their brethren, who would be killed as they were, was completed." **Revelation 6:9-11**

We are instructed not to pray that prayer because of the frailty of our flesh, meaning we would be seeking unrighteous vengeance, which belongs only to the Lord. These saints that died during the tribulation are only in spirit form without their bodies that have yet to be resurrected. Yet their souls are present before the Lord under the altar of incense, and their prayer is offered directly to the Father without a mediator. This can happen because they are now residents of heaven in perfect unity with the will of the heavenly Father. Note that God tells them to wait because the fullness of time has not yet come for Him to righteously pour out His wrath upon the earth. There are others who He wants saved. That's the answer, beloved. God wants more people saved, and He will execute judgment in His perfect time. No one will be able to claim that God was unjust. That's exactly what Peter said.

[8] But, beloved, do not forget this one thing, that with the Lord one day is as a thousand years, and a thousand years as one day. [9] The Lord is not slack concerning His promise, as some count slackness, but is longsuffering toward us, not willing that any should perish but that all should come to repentance. [10] But the day of the Lord will come as a thief in the night, in which the heavens will pass away with a great noise, and the elements will melt with fervent heat; both the earth and the works that are in it will be burned up. [11] Therefore, since all these things will be dissolved, what manner of persons ought you to be in holy conduct and godliness, [12] looking for and hastening the coming of the day of God, because of which the heavens will be dissolved, being on fire, and the elements will melt with fervent heat? [13] Nevertheless we, according to His promise, look for new heavens and a new earth in which righteousness dwells. **2 Peter 3:8-13**

Peter said the same thing to us on earth as the Lord said to the saints under the altar—wait. I am in the saving business and desire that none perish. The prayers of the saints from the fifth seal mark the end of man's ungodly reign over the earth as the Father prepares to unleash His wrath upon the ungodly. We see this expressly in the sixth seal as the Lord's anger sets off cosmic disturbances, and the wrath of God is unsealed.

From chapters 4 through 7, notice how there was the sound of rejoicing, singing, loud worship, and thundering voices that aroused the inhabitants of heaven into a crescendo praise. It was so loud that it shook the heavens. Then, suddenly, as the Lamb of God opens the seventh seal, silence, absolute, complete, and utter silence.

You ask: What happened? What could possibly take the thunderous praise of myriad of angels and billions of saints and cause them all to go deafly silent?

After Jesus broke the seventh seal, and the inhabitants of heaven saw what was written on the scroll when it was unfurled. They saw the wrath of God, which had never been revealed in its fulness from the beginning of creation until this time. Now they finally understood why the Lord was so patient and desired that all be saved. We, too, should now understand why the Lord has been as longsuffering and merciful as we read what the wrath of God truly looks like when unleashed. This should motivate us even more, to publicize the gospel to the ends of the earth.

"¹ When He opened the seventh seal, there was silence in heaven for about half an hour. ² And I saw the seven angels who stand before God, and to them were given seven trumpets. ³ Then another angel, having a golden censer, came and stood at the altar. He was given much incense, that he should offer it with the prayers of all the saints upon the golden altar which was before the throne. ⁴ And the smoke of the incense, with the prayers of the saints, ascended before God from the angel's hand. ⁵ Then the angel took the censer, filled it with fire from the altar, and threw it to the earth. And there were noises, thunderings, lightnings, and an earthquake." **Revelation 8:1-5**

Notice that the angel with the golden censer, which was similarly carried by the Levitical priest, took incense mixed with the prayers of all the saints. Finally, all the prayers of the saints will be answered at once, as the Lord GOD reacts, with righteous indignation, when smoke of prayer filled incense rise before His throne. There will no longer be any delay in the outpouring of God's wrath. All earth dwellers are now under the divinely appointed condemnation of the Lord. No one from this point ever repents although salvation is offered until the end of the great tribulation.

"⁵ Then the angel I had seen standing on the sea and on the land raised his right hand to heaven. ⁶ And he swore by him who lives for ever and ever, who created the heavens and all that is in them, the earth and all that is in it, and the sea and all that is in it, and said, "There will be no more delay! ⁷ But in the days when the seventh angel is about to sound his trumpet, the mystery of God will be accomplished, just as he announced to his servants the prophets." **Revelation 10:5-7**

The full force of the wrath of God envelopes the temple, and no one, not even the saints and angels, can stand in His presence. Therefore, the Holy One of Israel cloaks Himself with the shekinah glory, and no one behold Him lest they be consumed.

"¹ Then I saw another sign in heaven, great and marvelous: seven angels having the seven last plagues, for in them the wrath of God is complete. ² And I saw something like a sea of glass mingled with fire, and those who have the victory over the beast, over his image and over his mark and over the number of his name, standing on the sea of glass, having harps of God. ³They sing the song of Moses, the servant of God, and the song of the Lamb, saying: "Great and marvelous are Your works, Lord God Almighty! Just and true are Your ways, O King of the saints! ⁴ Who shall not fear You, O Lord, and glorify Your name? For You alone are holy.

For all nations shall come and worship before You, For Your judgments have been manifested." [5] After these things I looked, and behold, the temple of the tabernacle of the testimony in heaven was opened. [6] And out of the temple came the seven angels having the seven plagues, clothed in pure bright linen, and having their chests girded with golden bands. [7] Then one of the four living creatures gave to the seven angels seven golden bowls full of the wrath of God who lives forever and ever. [8] The temple was filled with smoke from the glory of God and from His power, and no one was able to enter the temple till the seven plagues of the seven angels were completed." **Revelation 15**

Prior to the Church arrival in heaven and the pouring out of God's wrath, the Father gave the Son a task which was to inspect the Church while they sojourn in the world declaring the gospel. We will begin with a brief overview then discuss the commendations and condemnations that the Lord gave from his inspection of the Church. Note that this is not meant to be an exhaustive study as a whole book could be written on the Lord's message to the seven churches and how they relate to the parables of Matthew 13. Today, our purpose is to simply look at the overview and outcome of the Lord's inspection of each church. The Lord's inspection is broken down into several categories:

1. Approximate periodic timeframe
2. Period in history
3. Jesus' description of Himself
4. Commendations
5. Condemnations
6. Exhortation

7. Judgment
8. Promise to overcomer

Revelation chapter 1 opens with the revealing of the trinitarian nature of the One true God. In verses 4 and 5, John presents greetings from the Father- grace, and peace; from the Spirit presenting our petitions before the Father's throne; and from Lord Jesus Christ, who is our faithfulness, our life, our Savior, and our King.

The Lord instructs John to write three things:

1. What he has seen,
2. Things that are happening now, and
3. Things that are to come.

What John saw was the glorified Christ in all His majesty, the majesty that He possessed with the Father and the Holy Spirit before He created the heavens and the earth and all the living creators therein.

"[12] I turned around to see the voice that was speaking to me. And when I turned, I saw seven golden lampstands, [13] and among the lampstands was someone like a son of man, dressed in a robe reaching down to his feet and with a golden sash around his chest. [14] The hair on his head was white like wool, as white as snow, and his eyes were like blazing fire. [15] His feet were like bronze glowing in a furnace, and his voice was like the sound of rushing waters. [16] In his right hand he held seven stars, and coming out of his mouth was a sharp, double-edged sword. His face was like the sun shining in all its brilliance. [17] When I saw him, I fell at his feet as though dead. Then he placed his right hand on me" **Revelation 1:12-17**

The things which are, are listed in verses 12 and 13 above, Jesus walking among the seven golden lampstands, which represents the completed body of Christ, the Church. The seven stars are the pastors of the churches. Each of the seven churches was in Asia Minor, which is modern-day Turkey. Note that these were actual, historical churches. However, there were more than seven churches in Asia Minor. By some estimates, there were between 10 to 20 house churches with no more than 100 members each. These seven were chosen for two specific reasons,

1. They represented the types of churches that perennially exist throughout the church age.
2. They represented the periodic timeline of the church age.

You say: I do not fully comprehend those two descriptions.

Then allow me to clarify. I have included a chart that depicts the periodic timeline of the church age and the age associated with each church.

The perennial nature of the church means that each type of church is living during each of the seven church ages listed in the chart below, including today and concluding with the rapture. For those who are new Christians who have never heard of the rapture, it is given to us by type in the Old Testament and by prophecy in the New Testament.

In the Old Testament, Enoch the prophet, the seventh generation from Adam, was raptured prior to the Lord sending the flood upon the earth. Noah and family witnessed the wrath of God; yet, they were protected from the flood. Enoch represented the church, and Noah represented Israel. Enoch remained in heaven while Noah repopulated the earth.

"[21] When Enoch had lived 65 years, he became the father of Methuselah. [22] After he became the father of Methuselah, Enoch walked faithfully with God 300 years and had other sons and daughters. [23] Altogether, Enoch lived a total of 365 years. [24] Enoch walked faithfully with God; then he was no more, because God took him away." **Genesis 5:21-24**

Apostle Paul provided two prophecies concerning the rapture of the church. The more popular being in 1 Thessalonians 4:13-18. The Thessalonian believers became concerned when fellow believers began to die because Paul had taught them that Jesus was to return to remove the church prior to the "day of the Lord" or the tribulation. Some fake believers began telling them that they were in the day of the Lord and had missed the rapture. Paul wrote to them to bring peace and comfort to their hearts as the promise made by the Lord would stand.

"[13] Brothers and sisters, we do not want you to be uninformed about those who sleep in death, so that you do not grieve like the rest of mankind, who have no hope. [14] For we believe that Jesus died and rose again, and so we believe that God will bring with Jesus those who have fallen asleep in him. [15] According to the Lord's word, we tell you that we who are still alive, who are left until the coming of the Lord, will certainly not precede those who have fallen asleep. [16] For the Lord himself will come down from heaven, with a loud command, with the voice of the archangel and with the trumpet call of God, and the dead in Christ will rise first. [17] After that, we who are still alive and are left will be caught up together with them in the clouds to meet the Lord in the air. And so we will be with the Lord forever. [18] Therefore encourage one another with these words." **1 Thessalonians 4:13-18**

The second reference is found in 1 Corinthians 15:50-54. Essentially, the same thing was happening to the church at Corinth. This time, members of the church were saying there wasn't going to be a resurrection, much less a rapture. Paul had to correct their theology by assuring them that not only will we be raised from the dead, but some will not go by way of the valley of the shadow of death.

"[50] I declare to you, brothers and sisters, that flesh and blood cannot inherit the kingdom of God, nor does the perishable inherit the imperishable. [51] Listen, I tell you a mystery: We will not all sleep, but we will all be changed — [52] in a flash, in the twinkling of an eye, at the last trumpet. For the trumpet will sound, the dead will be raised imperishable, and we will be changed. [53] For the perishable must clothe itself with the imperishable, and the mortal with immortality. [54] When the perishable has been clothed with the imperishable, and the mortal with immortality, then the saying that is written will come true: "Death has been swallowed up in victory." **1 Corinthians 15:50-54**

The periodical nature of the church simply means that each of the seven churches represented a distinct historical period whereby certain events transpired that was replicated by the description the Lord gave from His assessment of the church. We will see this more clearly as we discuss each church and church age. Before we commence our discussions of the individual churches, let's look at the meaning of their names.

THE CHURCH AGE CHART

Correlation with the Kingdom Parables - Prophecies of the Church Age

The Sower and the Seed Matthew 13:1-23	The Wheat and the Tares Matthew 13:24-30, 36-43	The Mustard Seed Matthew 13:31-32	The Leaven Matthew 13:33	The Hidden Treasure Matthew 13:44	The Pearl of Great Price Matthew 13:45-46	The Drag Net Matthew 13:47-50
		The Things Which Are - The Seven Churches				
Ephesus Revelation 2:1-7	Smyrna Revelation 2:8-11	Pergamos Revelation 2:12-17	Thyatira Revelation 2:18-29	Sardis Revelation 3:1-6	Philadelphia Revelation 3:7-13	Laodicea Revelation 3:14-22
First Church Age 33 - 100 AD Death of Christ 1st & 2nd Persecution By Rome	Second Church Age 100 - 312 AD The Roman Caesars 2nd - 10th Persecutions By Rome	Third Church Age 312 - 590 AD Roman Emperor Constantine converts to "Christianity" Birth of the Catholic Church The Political Church	Fourth Church Age 590 - 1517 AD Dark Ages The Idolatrous Catholic Church	Fifth Church Age 1517 - 1750 AD Reformation Protestantism Martin Luther	Sixth Church Age 1750 - 1925 AD Missionary Movement	Seventh Church Age 1925 - Present - Tribulation Apostate Church

1. Ephesus means—the desired one
2. Smyrna means—Myrrh, Death
3. Pergamos means—Mixed marriage
4. Thyatira means—Semiramis (introduction of idols in the church)
5. Sardis means—Remnant
6. Philadelphia means—Brotherly love
7. Laodicea means—People rule

The church at Ephesus was believed to be the most spiritual church due to the amount of time the Apostle Paul spent there, approximately three years. This church was also pastored by Tychicus, Timothy, the Apostle John, and attended by Mary. John served there until Emperor Domitian had him arrested and exiled to the isle of Patmos, where he received the Revelation from the Lord.

Let's look at what the Lord had to say concerning the churches.

Ephesus the loveless church (Revelations 2:1-7). What Jesus wants most from the church at Ephesus is for them to love Jesus the most.

Approximate periodic timeframe for the church of Ephesus:

1. AD 70–170.

Period in history

1. Early Church.

Jesus' description of Himself

1. The One who holds the seven stars in His right hand,

2. He who walks in the midst of the seven golden lampstands.

Commendations

1. I know your works—confirms that they have fruit, some 30, some 60, some 100-fold
2. Labor—they pursued his will
3. Patience—they waited on the Lord
4. Cannot bear evil—practiced holiness
5. Tested deceivers—had discernment and held firm to the apostles' doctrine
6. Persevered—endured hardship
7. Not become weary—walked by faith and zeal for truth
8. Hate the Nicolaitans—would not allow a priesthood to rule over the people, Nico means "one who rules or conquers," laos means "the people." Therefore, Nicolaitans means "ones that would rule over the people," a priesthood.

Condemnations

1. Left first love—life has become crowded, lost focus on Christ, service became mechanical instead of a labor of love.

Exhortation

1. Remember
2. Repent
3. Return

Judgment

1. Remove your lampstand—bring an end to the Ephesian church

Promise to overcomer

1. Access to the tree of life

Smyrna the persecuted church (Revelations 2:8-11). They loved Jesus to death.

Approximate periodic timeframe for the church of Smyrna:

1. AD 170–312

Period in history

1. Ten (10) Empirical Roman persecutions

Jesus' description of Himself

1. The First and the Last,
2. He who was dead (the cross) and came to life (the resurrection)

Commendations

1. Know your works—confirms fruitfulness
2. Tribulation—persecuted
3. Poverty—but rich toward Christ
4. Identified deceivers—Discernment

Condemnations

1. None

Exhortation

1. Fear not
2. Remain faithful even unto death
3. I will resurrect you

Judgment

1. None

Promise to overcomer

1. Crown of life
2. Avoid second death—spiritual death in the lake of fire

Pergamos the compromising church (Revelations 2:12-17) What Jesus wants most is that the church at Pergamum separate themselves from sin.

Commendations

1. Know your works—confirms fruitfulness
2. Knows dwelling place—the God that sees me
3. Hold fast Christ's name—love Christ
4. Keep the faith—faithful
5. Martyr—persecuted even unto death

Condemnations

1. Doctrine of Balaam—mixed marriages, believers with unbelievers who lead them astray from the Lord. The Israelite men married the Moabite women, which was prohibited by God because they were idol worshippers and sexually immoral.

2. Doctrine of Nicolaitans—commencement of a hierarchy priesthood to rule over the people. This was never God's intent for the body of Christ as we are all priests.

Exhortation

1. None

Judgment

1. Repent
2. Will quickly fight against those who distort his word

Promise to overcomer

1. Hidden manner—spiritual bread of life that the world cannot see or receive
2. White stone—invitation to the wedding supper of the Lamb

   Thyatira the corrupt church (Revelations 2:18-29) What Jesus wants most is for the church at Thyatira to unfriend the world.

Approximate periodic timeframe for the church of Ephesus:

1. AD 606–1520

Period in history

1. The Dark Ages when the Roman Catholic "church" priesthood ruled over the people

Jesus' description of Himself

1. The One who has eyes like a flame of fire,

2. He who has feet like fine brass

Commendations

1. Know your works—confirms fruitfulness
2. Love—for Christ and believers
3. Service—faith works through love
4. Faith—acted upon the word
5. Patience—wait upon the Lord
6. Increase in works—spiritual growth

Condemnations

1. Jezebel—tolerated sexual immorality and idolatry

Exhortation

1. Hold on, be patient

Judgment

1. Jezebel and her children will go through the great tribulation
2. Kill her children with death (second death—lake of fire)
3. Those who participate in her immorality will be sick in their bodies

Promise to the overcomer

1. Rest
2. Rule with Jesus in the Millennium
3. Morning star the promise of the rapture
   Sardis the dead church (Revelation 3:1-6) What Jesus wants most is that they have an overflowing Spirit-filled life.

Approximate periodic timeframe for the church of Ephesus:

1. AD 1520–1750.

Period in history

1. The reformation church movement started by Martin Luther

Jesus' description of Himself

1. The One who has the seven Spirits of God,
2. He who has the seven stars.

Commendations

1. Know your works—confirms fruitfulness

Condemnations

1. Have a name that is alive, but you are dead

Exhortation

1. Be watchful
2. Build upon most holy faith that remains
3. Those who are truly faithful, hold on

Judgment

1. Works not perfect
2. Sin unto death (physical)
3. Those who participate in her immorality will be sick in their bodies

Promise to the overcomer

1. Remember the words received and heard

2. Walk with Jesus dressed in his righteousness
   3. Promise never to remove name from book of Life
   4. Confess before the Father and introduction to the angels

   Philadelphia the faithful church (Revelation 3:7-13).
   What Jesus wants most is that they continue to be faithful.

Approximate periodic timeframe for the church of Philadelphia:

   1. AD 1750–1900

Period in history

   1. The modern age of missionary zeal

Jesus' description of Himself

   1. The One who is Holy,
   2. He who is true
   3. He who has the key of David. Having the key of David gives the possessor the control of David's domain, such as becoming the king of Israel and Jerusalem

Commendations

   1. Know your works—confirms fruitfulness
   2. Little strength, speaking of the size of the body
   3. Kept my words—openly showed the evidence of saving faith in obedience
   4. Not denied Christ—openly confessed Christ
   5. Kept command to persevere—lived as sojourners and strangers, heavenly-minded

Condemnations

   1. None

Exhortation

> 1. Enemies defeated
> 2. Loved by Christ
> 3. Open doors for missionary work
> 4. Promise of the rapture
> 5. Hold fast what you have
> 6. Keep your crown

Judgment

> 1. None

Promise to the overcomer

> 1. Pillar in God's temple
> 2. Will live in God's presence
> 3. Sealed by God
> 4. Dwell with God
> 5. Identified with God

Laodicea the lukewarm church (Revelation 3:14-22) What Jesus wants most from the church at Laodicea is a representative crucified lifestyle.

Approximate periodic timeframe for the church of Ephesus:

> 1. AD 1900–present

Period in history

> 1. The final apostate church where demons will come to lodge

Jesus' description of Himself
- 1. The Amen,
- 2. He who is the Faithful and True Witness
- 3. The One through whom God created all things

Commendations
- 1. Know your works—confirms some fruitfulness

Condemnations
- 1. Warm—stagnant, serving themselves and without Jesus they are:
  - a. Wretched—still in their sins
  - b. Miserable—no hope
  - c. Poor—unable to purchase salvation
  - d. Blind—cannot see the truth in Jesus
  - e. Naked—self-righteous

Exhortation
- 1. Cold—refreshing, start encouraging the saints
- 2. Hot—reinvigorating, start witnessing the loss
- 3. Buy without cost—gold, become heavenly minded
- 4. White garments—this is the outer garment rewarded for faithful service
- 5. Eye salve—understanding open to spiritual truth
- 6. Be zealous to repent

Judgment
- 1. Rebuke—correct theology

2. Chasten—from sickness to death
3. Knock—loss of fellowship

Promise to the overcomer

1. Promise to live in the New Jerusalem where the throne of God will be located

   Below is a quick look at how the seven churches align with the parables of Matthew 13. I have future plans, by the grace of God, to write extensively on this topic.

   Ephesus is the Sower of seed church.

   Smyrna has both wheat and tares, believers along with unbelievers who look and act like believers actively attending church services,

   Pergamos is the true church with a small beginning that grows into this monstrosity that the birds, which represent demons, are nesting in its branches.

   Thyatira is the church that began with the pure gospel, then it allowed that woman, Jezebel, to insert three measures leaven, false doctrine until the whole church was infected. By the way, I believe that the three measures of leaven are the major Christian denominations, Catholicism, Eastern Orthodoxy, and the Reformation churches.

   Sardis is the field that was purchased after the treasure was hidden.

   Philadelphia is the precious pearl of great price that will continue to be on display by the Lord throughout all eternity.

The Laodicean church is the dragnet pulled from the sea of humanity that has every type of fish (good and evil) imaginable and is so corrupt that only the holy angels are trusted by God to separate them from the world.

CHAPTER 2

DISCIPLINING THE CHURCH

Now that we have established our position as believers and children of God, let us turn our focus to the progression of the Lord's discipline of his children by looking at the church at Corinth. They were probably the most undisciplined church in all the kingdom. Well, Laodicea gave them a run for the gold medal for the most undisciplined church of the age.

What was happening in the church at Corinth?

Background and Setting

The city of Corinth was located in southern Greece, in what was the Roman province of Achaia, ca. 45 miles west of Athens. This lower part, the Peloponnesus, is connected to the rest of Greece by a 4-mile-wide isthmus, which is bounded on the east by the Saronic Gulf and on the west by the Gulf of Corinth.

The Isthmian games, one of the two most famous athletic events of that day (the other being the Olympian Games, which took place in Olympia, Greece), was hosted by Corinth, causing more people traffic. Even by the pagan standards of its own culture, Corinth became so morally corrupt that its very name became synonymous with debauchery and moral depravity. The Isthmian games athletes participated in the nude. To "Corinthianize" came to represent gross immorality and drunken debauchery. In **1 Cor. 6:9-10**, Paul lists some of the specific sins for which the city was noted and formerly characterized many believers in the church there. Tragically, some of the worst sins were still found among some church members. One of those sins, incest, was condemned even by most pagan Gentiles.

"[1] It is actually reported that there is sexual immorality among you, and such sexual immorality as is not even named among the Gentiles that a man has his father's wife!" **1 Corinthians 5:1**

Like most ancient Greek cities, Corinth had an acropolis (lit. "a high city"), which rose 2,000 feet and was used both for defense and for worship. The most prominent edifice on the acropolis was a temple to Aphrodite, the Greek goddess of love and fertility. Some 1,000 priestesses, who were "religious" prostitutes, lived and worked there without clothing and came down into the city in the evening to offer their services to male citizens and foreign visitors.

Unfortunately, the church sat on a plateau between the two sites, the temple above and the arena below, both in plain view.

The church in Corinth was founded by Paul on his second missionary journey (see **Acts 18**), ministering there for 18 months, where he was assisted by two Jewish believers, Priscilla and Aquila, with whom he lived for a while and who were fellow tradesmen, tentmakers.

Unable to fully break with the culture from which it came, the church at Corinth was exceptionally factional, showing its carnality and immaturity. After the gifted Apollos had ministered in the church for some time, a group of his admirers established a clique and had little to do with the rest of the church. Another group developed that was loyal to Paul, another claimed special allegiance to Peter (Cephas), and still another to Christ alone.

"¹⁰ Now I plead with you, brethren, by the name of our Lord Jesus Christ, that you all speak the same thing, and that there be no divisions among you, but that you be perfectly joined together in the same mind and in the same judgment. ¹¹ For it has been declared to me concerning you, my brethren, by those of Chloe's household, that there are contentions among you. ¹² Now I say this, that each of you says, "I am of Paul," or "I am of Apollos," or "I am of Cephas," or "I am of Christ." ¹³ Is Christ divided? Was Paul crucified for you? Or were you baptized in the name of Paul?" **1 Corinthians 1:10-13**

The most serious problem of the Corinthian church was worldliness, an unwillingness to divorce completely, the culture around them. Most of the believers could not consistently separate themselves from their old, selfish, immoral, and pagan ways.

It became necessary for Paul to write to correct this and command the faithful Christians not only to break fellowship with the disobedient and unrepentant members but to put those members out of the church.

"⁹ I wrote to you in my epistle not to keep company with sexually immoral people. ¹⁰ Yet I certainly did not mean with the sexually immoral people of this world, or with the covetous, or extortioners, or idolaters, since then you would need to go out of the world. ¹¹ But now I have written to you not to keep company with anyone named a brother, who is sexually immoral, or covetous, or an idolater, or a reviler, or a drunkard, or an extortioner not even to eat with such a person. ¹² For what have I to do with judging those also who are outside? Do you not judge those who are inside? ¹³ But those who are outside God judges. Therefore "put away from yourselves the evil person." **1 Corinthians 5:9-13**

Our focus will be on the disciplinary actions taken by the Lord concerning the solemn celebration of the Lord's supper.

For whenever you eat this bread and drink this cup, you proclaim the Lord's death until he comes. So then, whoever eats the bread or drinks the cup of the Lord in an unworthy manner will be guilty of sinning against the body and blood of the Lord. Everyone ought to examine themselves before they eat of the bread and drink from the cup. For those who eat and drink without discerning the body of Christ eat and drink judgment on themselves. That is why **many** among you are **weak** and **sick**, and a number of you have **fallen asleep**. But if we were more discerning with regard to ourselves, we would not come under such judgment. Nevertheless, when we are judged in this way by the Lord, **we are being disciplined so that we will not be finally condemned with the world.**" **1 Cor. 11:26-32**

Therefore, by reason of the scriptures above, we should understand that God's children are disciplined while the earth dwellers (the world's and Satan's children) are condemned. Believers are kept from being consigned to hell, not only by divine decree,

"²⁴ Now to Him who is able to keep you from stumbling, and to present you faultless before the presence of His glory with exceeding joy, ²⁵ To God our Savior, who alone is wise, be glory and majesty, dominion and power, both now and forever. Amen." **Jude 1:24-25**

"³ Blessed be the God and Father of our Lord Jesus Christ, who according to His abundant mercy has begotten us again to a living hope through the resurrection of Jesus Christ from the dead, ⁴ to an inheritance incorruptible and undefiled and that does not fade away, reserved in heaven for you, ⁵ who are kept by the power of God through faith for salvation ready to be revealed in the last time." **1 Peter 1:3-5**

But by divine intervention. The Lord (the Good Shepard **Ps. 23**) chastens (with His rod and staff **Ps. 23**) to drive His children (sheep **Jn. 10**) back to righteous behavior (provisional sanctification **1 Cor. 11:32**). The worst offenders were removed from the place of fruit-bearing, planet earth; in other words, God killed them. The Lord's chastisement is threefold:

Progression of discipline for Corinthian believers

1. Weak—lacking strength in the joints (paralyzed), frail, maimed
2. Sick—mental or physical illness
3. Fall asleep—physical death

CHAPTER 3

THE SIN UNTO DEATH

Death?

Yes, death. While it may seem odd or extreme to most believers, it is taught throughout the entire word of God. It is not stated in the exact terms the Apostle John described. However, it is evidenced throughout the scriptures. We will explore episodes in both the Testaments.

"¹⁶If you see any brother or sister commit a sin that does not lead to death, you should pray, and God will give them life. I refer to those whose sin does not lead to death. **There is a sin that leads to death (physical death)**. I am not saying that you should pray about that. ¹⁷All wrongdoing is sin, and there is sin that does not lead to death" **1 John 5:16-17**

The Holy Spirit inspired John to write that warning to believers. What is this sin unto death?

The first thing we need to understand about this "sin unto death" is that it's not "the" sin unto death but "a" sin unto death. The difference, it can be any sin that a believer commits at any time. The account of Ananias and Sapphira, his wife, is the perfect example in **Acts 5**. They were both believers; yet, they attempted to deceive the early church leaders concerning an offering, and it cost them their lives. What was their sin? Peter said that they lied to the Holy Ghost, who is God.

Do you understand that every sin committed is against God? Though we ourselves and others, such as family, neighbors, friends, etc., are impacted, all sins are lawlessness, which is rebellion against the holiness of God. How many times have we told the Lord that we will do or say something only not to do or complete the task? God has not killed each of us for lying. Therefore, lying in and of itself cannot be "the" sin unto death. By the way, I am not advocating for lying, nor am I justifying lying, as it is sin and one of the six (6) sins listed in **Proverbs 6:16-19** that God said he hates.

"[16] These six things the LORD hates, yes, seven are an abomination to Him: [17] A proud look, A lying tongue, hands that shed innocent blood, [18] A heart that devises wicked plans, feet that are swift in running to evil, [19] A false witness who speaks lies, and one who sows discord among brethren." **Proverbs 6:16-19**

The point here is that the lie was told at a specific time, to a specific individual, about a specific circumstance by certain people who had a particular level of Christian maturity. These factors together made the sin of lying by Ananias and Sapphira, in God's eyes, worthy of the death penalty. By the way, exaggeration is lying.

This was the early church, and God had to keep out any impurity (sins) that would stunt its growth. The church may not have survived if sin would have been allowed to permeate at this stage in church history. Therefore, in his sovereign wisdom, God protected it.

I will now site a few other episodes from both the Old and New Testaments.

Old Testament

Numbers 20 & 27 Aaron and Moses—God took both their lives for striking the rock twice, thereby failing to sanctify the Lord before the people by not performing the task exactly as instructed. God told Moses to speak to the rock to provide water for the children of Israel. The rock represented Jesus after the resurrection, the fountain of living water. Striking the rock meant judgment, but that was carried out at the cross and through the ceremonial animal blood sacrifices, which could only be carried out by the high priest, Aaron. Christ will never be judged for sin after the resurrection, for Jesus, once for all times, offered the perfect sacrifice upon the cross, being evident by the bodily resurrection of our Savior. What was Moses' and Aaron's sin? **Blatant disobedience,** because they did not trust in the Lord enough to honor Him as holy in the sight of the Israelites.

1 Kings 13 The unnamed prophet—The Lord instructed the prophet to convey a message to King Jeroboam of Israel, then return to Judah on a pathway different from the pathway taken leading to his destination. The prophet was also instructed to not eat bread or drinking water in the nation of Israel. However, an old Israel prophet talked him into doing both. The Lord sent a lion to kill him on the way back to Judah. What was his sin? **Compromise**, he obeyed man rather than God.

1 Chronicles 13 Uzzah the priest—David was attempting to bring the ark of God from Kiriath Jearim (Baalah) to Jerusalem. The oxen pulling the cart upon which the ark sat stumbled, and Uzzah (one of the priests assisting with the move) stretched out his hand and touched the ark to keep it from falling, and the Lord killed Uzzah on the spot. What was his sin? **Irreverence**: the ark represented God's presence. Sinful man cannot enter the presence of the Lord without a blood sacrifice, and under the law, only the High Priest could enter behind the veil, once each year but only after providing a sin offering, taking a ceremonial bath, and changing into the High Priest garments. Each one of these acts represents our Savior, the Lord Jesus Christ. Jesus is our High Priest who offered himself upon the cross to God, His and our Father. **Hebrews chapters 4-8**. Out of His pierced side flowed blood and water, blood to redeem and water to cleanse (our ceremonial bath). Note that David and the priests were already in disobedience to the Lord as it was commanded that the priests use the ark rings with golden poles to carry the ark upon their shoulders. They placed the ark on a cart and let animals carry it. Do you still think the oxen stumbling was a misstep? I do not.

"³⁴But one of the soldiers pierced His side with a spear, and immediately blood and water came out." **John 19:34**

Being regenerated by the Spirit of Christ, "⁴But when the kindness and love of God our Savior appeared, ⁵ he saved us, not because of righteous things we had done, but because of his mercy. He saved us through the washing of rebirth and renewal by the Holy Spirit, ⁶ whom he poured out on us generously through Jesus Christ our Savior, ⁷ so that, having been justified by his grace, we might become heirs having the hope of eternal life." **Titus 3:4-7**

The Father issued us (imputed) the white robe of righteousness, which is worn by our risen Savior, Christ Jesus the Lord of glory at the resurrection. This is our inner garment. "⁵The one who is victorious (overcomer) will, like them, be dressed in white. I will never blot out the name of that person from the book of life but will acknowledge that name before my Father and his angels. **Revelation 3:5**

Below is a description of our outer garment, which we will wear as a reward for faithful obedience to the Lord while here on the earth.

"⁶Hallelujah! For our Lord God Almighty reigns. ⁷ Let us rejoice and be glad and give him glory! For the wedding of the Lamb has come, and his bride has made herself ready. ⁸ Fine linen, bright and clean, was given her to wear." (**Fine linen stands for the righteous acts** of God's holy people.)" **Revelation 19:6-8**

Here is New Testament evidence of "sin unto death."

Acts 5 Ananias and Sapphira—see details above. When we get to heaven, they will tell us how stupid it was to **lie** to God.

1 Cor. 5 Unnamed believer—This believer was committing sexual immorality that even most unbelievers would not do. He was having sexual relations with his father's wife (stepmother). Paul said, in the power of the Lord, that this person should be handed over to Satan for the destruction of the flesh (death), yet he is still saved. This was to keep the sinning believer from continually dishonoring the Lord and the Church by committing such an unconscionable sin. What was his sin? **Sexual perversion**: note that this man sincerely repented, thereby escaping the death penalty, and was later restored full fellowship by the Lord and the Church. You can read about that in **2 Cor. 2**.

1 Cor. 11 Corinthian believers—Church members were arriving at the solemn communion feast drunk, hungry, and with unrepentant overt sins. This lack of discernment caused the Lord to kill many of the believers while others were judged with a less severe punishment; some became weak, and others were sick. What was their sin? **Insolence**: the vast lack of discernment concerning the Lord's supper, which represented the most hallowed event in all eternity to a holy God. It is one thing for an unbeliever to conduct themselves in such a manner; it is totally different when a believer who knows the gospel, the only mode of salvation, to commit such an insult and sin.

I realize that this may come as a shock to some of you to read that the Lord actually "kills" (take home) his children as a disciplinary action. However, we must take care to remember that the Lord is high and exalted, seated upon His throne, glorious in holiness, majestic in glory, righteous in all His ways, His judgments are just and true.

As the scripture says, "[20]But who are you, a human being, to talk back to God? "Shall what is formed say to the one who formed it, 'Why did you make me like this?'" **Romans 9:20**

"[37]Now I, Nebuchadnezzar, praise and exalt and glorify the King of heaven, because everything he does is right and all his ways are just. And those who walk in pride he is able to humble." **Daniel 4:37**

"[4]For the word of the LORD is right; and all his works are done in truth. [5]He loveth righteousness and judgment: the earth is full of the goodness of the LORD. **Psalms 33:4-5**

"[4]He is the Rock, his work is perfect: for all his ways are judgment: a God of truth and without iniquity, just and right is he." **Deuteronomy 32:4**

"[39]See now that I, even I, am he, and there is no god with me: **I kill, and I make alive; I wound, and I heal**: neither is there any that can deliver out of my hand." **Deuteronomy 32:39**

That should provide clarity on the "sin unto death."

CHAPTER 4

PROGRESSION OF THE LORD'S DISCIPLINE

Continuing with the progression of the Lord's discipline, we find this in the book of Hebrews:

"⁵And ye have forgotten the exhortation which speaks unto you as unto children, My son, **despise not thou the chastening of the Lord**, nor faint when thou art rebuked of him: ⁶For whom the Lord loveth he **chastens, and scourge every son whom he receives.**

⁷If you endure chastening, God deals with you as with sons; for what son is he whom the father chastens not? ⁸But if ye be without chastisement, whereof all are partakers, then are you bastards, and not sons. ⁹Furthermore, we have had fathers of our flesh which corrected us, and we gave them reverence: shall we not much rather be in subjection unto the Father of spirits, and live? ¹⁰For they verily for a few days chastened us after their own pleasure; but he (1) **for our profit**, that we might be (2)**partakers of his holiness.** ¹¹Now no chastening for the present seems to be joyous, but grievous: nevertheless, afterward it (3)**yields the peaceable** (4)**fruit of righteousness** unto them which are exercised thereby.

¹²"Wherefore lift up the a) **hands which hang down** (weak—paralyzed), ¹³and the b) **feeble knees** (sick); and make **straight paths for your feet** (i)(repentance), lest that which is c) **lame** (weak) be d) **turned out of the way** (physical death); but let it rather be healed (ii)(restored to proper fellowship)." **Heb. 12:5-13**

Progression of discipline for Hebrew believers

1. Hands that hang down by their sides—paralysis (weak)
2. Feeble knees (sick)
3. Lame (weak)
4. Turned out of the way (physical death)

Purpose of discipline (all believers)

a) For our good
b) To make us partakers of his holiness
c) We can have his peace
d) Walking in righteousness—purity of life

Produce of discipline (all believers)

i. Straightened pathways (repentance)
ii. Healing (restored fellowship and assurance)

Note that pretenders (fake believers) are not disciplined. Therefore, if you find yourself committing sins without conviction of conscience, without correction by the Holy Spirit, and without chastisement by the Lord Jesus, **then you can be certain that you are not saved.** Listen to the writer of Hebrews, "⁸But if ye be without chastisement, whereof all (believers) are partakers, **then are you illegitimate, and not sons.**" **Heb. 12:8**

Now that we have a clear understanding of God's view of believers versus unbelievers and illustrated from scripture the progression, purpose, and produce of the Lord's discipline of believers, let us conclude with the process.

Process of discipline (all believers)

1. Conviction—pressing on the heart
2. Confrontation—God challenges His children directly
3. Chastisement—God takes His children to the woodshed
4. Consummation—God meets out due punishment, even unto death

As mentioned in the principles outlined above, the best commentary on the Bible is the Bible. We have a vivid picture and contrast between the lives of David, a man after God's own heart, and Joseph, a picture of Christ—the Servant of the Lord. How did each man react when tempted by a woman, and how did God respond?

David and Bathsheba vs. Joseph and Potiphar's wife

II Sam. 11:1-2 tells us about David's temptation:

"**¹And it came to pass**, after the year was expired, at the time when kings go forth to battle, that David sent Joab, and his servants with him, and all Israel; and they destroyed the children of Ammon, and besieged Rabbah. But David tarried still at Jerusalem.

²**And it came to pass** in an evening tide, that David arose from off his bed, and walked upon the roof of the king's house: and from the roof he **saw** a woman washing herself; and the woman was very beautiful to **look** upon.

1. Did not participate in the battle—David removes his armor

2. Tarried still at Jerusalem—David became lazy
3. Arose from bed in an evening tide—David became idle

We are told twice in two verses "And it came to pass."

Whenever you see this phraseology in the word of God, you know that the Lord is speaking about a duration of time. Fortunately for us, we are told the duration in the same verse; "after the year was expired." We also note that when phrases or words are repeated within a few verses, they are for additional emphasis.

It is the slow progression of sin. David's idleness allowed him to notice things that he did not have time to notice before. He was supposed to go to war with his men dressed in his armor, but he did not. David was supposed to be on the battlefield, but he was in Jerusalem. Battles in those days typically take place early in the morning, but David was in bed until evening. There is no doubt that David had walked upon the roof of his house a thousand times and never noticed Bathsheba. Now observe what David did.

V2. David saw, then David looked

It is the classic trap of sin. Sin gets you to visualize as it subtly shoots a fiery image to your mind, encourages meditation thereupon, then motivates desire.

James 1:13-15 provides the steps a believer takes to commit sin:

"¹³Let no man say when he is tempted, I am tempted of God: for God cannot be tempted with evil, neither tempts he any man: ¹⁴But every man is **tempted**, when he is **drawn away** of his own **lust**, and **enticed**. ¹⁵Then when lust hath **conceived**, it bringeth forth **sin**: and sin, when it is finished, bringeth forth **death**."

1. Tempted
2. Drawn away
3. Lust
4. Enticed
5. Conceived (indulge)
6. Sin
7. Death

These steps bring forth the loss of a life consecrated to God and forfeiture of heavenly rewards. Every believer has an obligation to repent during steps one through six. However, reaching step seven will have you repenting to the Lord face to face.

Gen. 3:6 "…and when the woman **saw** that the tree was good for food, and that it was **pleasant to the eyes**, and a tree to be **desired** to make on wise…"

Jesus said in **Mat. 5:28** "But I say unto you, that whosoever **looks** upon a woman **to lust** after her…"

Jesus did not say, see a woman, because if you have eyes and are not blind, then you see everything and everyone. However, you do not look upon them with desire.

David's idleness led to his chastisement. We read in II Sam. 11 & 12

1. David's plot to deceive—II Sam. 11: 4-12
2. David's plot to destroy—II Sam. 11: 13-27
3. David's plot to discharge—II Sam. 12: 1-5
4. David's plot disclosed—II Sam. 12: 6-21

Here are the four processes of discipline in action.

David was first convicted of his sin. Therefore, he attempted to deceive Uriah.

David was second confronted for his sin by the Lord, who sent Nathan the prophet to the palace.

David was third chastised for his sin, as detailed in Psalms 38 and 51, where he cries out in agony and remorse to the Lord.

"O Lord, rebuke me not in thy wrath: neither chastise me in thy hot displeasure. For **thine arrows stick fast in me**, and **thy hand press me sore**...neither is there **any rest in my bones** because of my sin...**my wounds stink and are corrupt** because of my foolishness. I am **troubled;** I go **mourning** all the day long. For **my loins are filled with a loathsome (*venereal*) disease**..." **Psalms 38**

The only reason David did not die is because he truly repented.

"And David said unto Nathan, I have sinned against the Lord. And Nathan said unto David, The Lord also hath put away thy sin; **THOU SHALT NOT DIE."** II Sam. 12:13

Beloved, had David not confessed his sin and the Lord had mercy, according to the law of Moses, he should have and would have died.

"Have mercy upon me, O God,...blot out my transgressions. Wash me thoroughly from mine iniquity...**For I acknowledge my transgressions** and my sin is ever before me...**Create in me a clean heart**, O God, and renew a right spirit within me. **Cast me not away** from thy presence and **take not thy Holy Spirit from me.** Restore unto me the **joy of thy salvation." Psalms 51**

Beloved, David was not talking about losing salvation, for he said to restore the **JOY** of thy salvation. Cast me not away, and taking the Holy Spirit meant physical death and the anointing of being king. David remembered what happened to Saul.

What were the (fourth process of discipline) consummations of David's sins?

1. The baby with Bathsheba dies.
2. David's son Amnon rapes his daughter, Tamer.
3. David's son and Tamer's brother Absalom, kills all Amnon's family.
4. Absalom rebels against his father David and publicly sleeps with his wives.
5. David's favorite son, Absalom, is killed.
6. There was no more peace during David's reign as his enemies were emboldened and attacked constantly.
7. David numbered the men of war, and God smote them.
8. Solomon became king and introduced idol worship to the nation.
9. Solomon's son, Rehoboam, loses ten tribes from the Davidic line.
10. The Davidic royal line returned to poverty by the time Jesus was born.

What a tragic price to pay! From the palace of King David to the stable of Christ. For what? One night of lustful pleasure. Beloved, there is pleasure in sin but sin, when it is finished, brings forth death. Do not be deceived, God is not mocked; for whatever a man sows, that shall he also reap.

By contrast, we will now look at the life of Joseph, who had purposed in his heart to obey the words of the Lord.

1. Consecration—a passionate desire to please the Lord
2. Communion—intimate fellowship with the Lord
3. Commendation—earthly and heavenly reward for walking with the Lord
4. Consummation—fulfilled life walking with the Lord

In Gen. 37 & 38, we learn of Joseph's betrayal by his brothers, like the Lord Jesus and the Jews. In chapter 39, Joseph is sold as a slave to an Egyptian. Though he was harassed and persecuted, Joseph purposed in his heart to serve the Lord. As a result:

1. The Lord was with him, and he was a prosperous man.
2. The Lord made all that he did to prosper.
3. Joseph faithfully served his new master.
4. The Lord blessed Joseph AND his master.

Now, keenly observe verse 7 of Gen. 39 as we read these words, "and it came to pass," that Potiphar's wife cast her eyes upon Joseph—she looked with desire. In verse 10, we read again, "and it came to pass," day after day, she desired Joseph. In verse 11, we read again, "and it came to pass," that Joseph was not idle, for he "went into the house **to do his business**"

Joseph's (1) consecration to the Lord:

⁸But he refused. "With me in charge," he told her, "**my master** does not concern himself with anything in the house; everything he owns he has entrusted to my care. ⁹ No one is greater in this house than I am. **My master** has withheld nothing from me except you, because you are his wife. How then could I **do such a wicked thing and sin against God?**" ¹⁰ And though she spoke to Joseph day after day, **he refused** to go to bed with her **or even be with her**.

¹¹ One day he went into the house to attend to his duties, and none of the household servants was inside. ¹² She caught him by his cloak and said, "Come to bed with me!" But he left his cloak in her hand and ran out of the house.

¹³ When she saw that he had left his cloak in her hand and had run out of the house, ¹⁴ she called her household servants. "Look," she said to them, "this Hebrew has been brought to us to make sport of us! He came in here to sleep with me, but I screamed. ¹⁵ When he heard me scream for help, he left his cloak beside me and ran out of the house."

¹⁶ She kept his cloak beside her until his master came home. ¹⁷ Then she told him this story: "That Hebrew slave you brought us came to me to make sport of me. ¹⁸ But as soon as I screamed for help, he left his cloak beside me and ran out of the house."

¹⁹ When his master heard the story his wife told him, saying, "This is how your slave treated me," he burned with anger. ²⁰ Joseph's master took him and put him in prison, the place where the king's prisoners were confined.

But while Joseph was there in the prison, **Genesis 39:8-20**

1. Joseph decided Gen. 39: 8
2. Joseph declined Gen. 39: 11
3. Joseph departed Gen. 39: 12
4. Joseph defamed Gen. 39: 14-20

Joseph's (2) communion with the Lord:

"the LORD was **with him**; he **showed him** kindness and **granted him** favor in the eyes of the prison warden." **Genesis 39:21**

1. The Lord protected Joseph Gen. 39: 21
2. The Lord showed Joseph pity Gen. 39: 21
3. The Lord gave Joseph privilege Gen. 39: 21

The Lord's three commendations for Joseph's faithfulness:

"So the warden put Joseph **in charge** of all those held in the prison, and he was **made responsible** for **all that was done** there." **Genesis 39:22**

1. The Lord gave Joseph provisions Gen. 39: 22
2. The Lord gave Joseph promotions Gen. 39: 22
3. The Lord caused Joseph to prosper Gen. 39: 22

The four consummations of Joseph's faithfulness:

[41] So Pharaoh said to Joseph, "I hereby **put you in charge** of the whole land of Egypt." [42] Then Pharaoh took his signet ring from his finger and put it on Joseph's finger. He dressed him in robes of fine linen and put a gold chain around his neck. [43] He had him ride in a chariot as his **second-in-command**, and people shouted before him, "Make way!" Thus he put him in charge of the whole land of Egypt.

[44] Then Pharaoh said to Joseph, "I am Pharaoh, **but without your word no one will lift hand or foot in all Egypt**." [45] Pharaoh gave Joseph the name Zaphenath-Paneah and gave him Asenath daughter of Potiphera, priest of On, to be his wife. And Joseph went throughout the land of Egypt.

[46] Joseph was thirty years old when he entered the service of Pharaoh king of Egypt. And Joseph went out from Pharaoh's

presence and traveled throughout Egypt. ⁴⁷ During the seven years of abundance the land produced plentifully. ⁴⁸ Joseph collected all the food produced in those seven years of abundance in Egypt and stored it in the cities. In each city he put the food grown in the fields surrounding it. ⁴⁹ Joseph stored up huge quantities of grain, like the sand of the sea; it was so much that he stopped keeping records because it was beyond measure. ⁵⁰ Before the years of famine came, two sons were born to Joseph by Asenath daughter of Potiphera, priest of On. ⁵¹ Joseph named his firstborn Manasseh and said, "It is because **God has made me forget all my trouble** and all my father's household." **Genesis 41:41-51**

1. The Lord gave Joseph a position Gen. 41: 41
2. The Lord gave Joseph power Gen. 41: 43-45
3. The Lord gave Joseph peace Gen. 41: 51

Closing out our study, we conclude that the Lord only disciplines and rewards his children, those that are true believers in Christ.

David looked.	Joseph forsook.
David lusted.	Joseph fled.
David conspired.	Joseph framed.
David convicted.	Joseph flourished.
David chastised.	Joseph feasted.

Which path will you choose?

The End.

BIBLIOGRAPHY

All Scripture references are from:

New King James Version (NKJV)

Publisher: Thomas Nelson

Copyright: All rights reserved

Build date: Tuesday, March 5, 2019

And

New International Version (NIV)

Publisher: Biblica

Copyright: © 1973, 1978, 1984, 2011 by Biblica, Inc.

Build date: Wednesday, October 23, 2019

ABOUT THE AUTHOR

Kevin Madison is an author, husband, and father who has walked faithfully with the Lord for over 28 years. The son of the late Pastor Leroy Phillips and Billie Mae Phillips, who raised their 13 children to love and fear the God of salvation and King of righteousness.

Modeling his study pattern after his former pastor, Carl Brown of Baton Rouge, LA, and current favorite pastors, Dr. John Barnett and John MacArthur, Kevin has become proficient at dissecting the scriptures verse by verse. Greatly impacted by his affection and love for the late Dr. J. Vernon McGee, who always challenged his listeners to study the entire word of God, Kevin has written many topical articles and yet to be published verse by verse commentaries on the Old Testament prophets. He is the author of several books, including *Predestined to Hell? Why Would a God Love Consign People to Hell FOREVER?* and *America - the Judgment of Sodom & Gomorrah*, and *The God that Loves and Hates*. He has several other upcoming titles soon to be published, including the much-anticipated title *Story of the Ages—God's Plan to Eliminate the Possibility of Sin*.

www.ingramcontent.com/pod-product-compliance
Lightning Source LLC
Chambersburg PA
CBHW020905080526
44589CB00011B/446